Turning Back the Darkness

TURNING BACK THE DARKNESS

*The Biblical Pattern
of Reformation*

RICHARD D. PHILLIPS

CROSSWAY BOOKS

A DIVISION OF
GOOD NEWS PUBLISHERS
WHEATON, ILLINOIS

First printing, 2002

Cover design: Josh Dennis

Printed in the United States of America

Library of Congress Cataloging-in-Publication Data
Phillips, Richard D. (Richard Davis), 1960-
 Turning back the darkness : the biblical pattern of reformation /
Richard D. Phillips.
  p. cm.
 Includes bibliographical references and index.
 ISBN 1-58134-398-1 (pbk. : alk. paper)
 1. Church renewal—Biblical teaching. I. Title.
BS680.C48 P48 2002
269—dc21   2002001696
                 CIP

15	14	13	12	11	10	09	08	07	06	05	04	03	02
15	14	13	12	11	10	9	8	7	6	5	4	3	2	1

To the memory of
James Montgomery Boice
pastor, reformer, mentor, and friend
ROMANS 11:36

and to
The Great Reformer
who stands amidst the lampstands,
seven stars within His hand
REVELATION 1:13, 16

TABLE OF CONTENTS

FOREWORD
R. C. Sproul

How easy it is to be trapped and enslaved by one's own traditions. Rarely is it doctrine that grips our consciences and causes us to take bold and inflexible stands for God. More often it is "love-lines"—strings that tether us to our own beloved teachers and mentors. If we love those who taught us, we are loath to hear anything contrary to the maxims these beloved teachers have passed on to us. Yet in every generation we face the leaven of the Pharisees, those who substituted their own human traditions for the Word of God. In the final analysis the only tradition that counts is the prophetic and apostolic tradition, for in that "giving over" we encounter nothing less and nothing more than the tradition of God.

I love the Reformed faith. I love it because I am convinced that it is the biblical faith. I admit that I have a fierce loyalty to the magisterial reformers Luther and Calvin; but that loyalty does not rest on a sanguine view of them that merely sees them as inspired. God forbid. I love them because, as Reformers, they constantly push me back to the Word itself.

The Reformers of the sixteenth century were not revolutionaries. A revolutionary is one who is engaged in revolt. A revolutionary wants a radical restructuring of current systems. In contrast, the Reformers sought not *new* forms, but a return to the purity of the original forms instituted by God. To *reform* presupposes a prior form that has been misshaped. To reform is to form again, to recapture the original.

What I most appreciate about this book is its focus. The eye of the writer is not fixed simply on our heroes from church history such as Luther and Calvin; nay, the focus is on the biblical pattern of reformation.

Rick Phillips demonstrates clearly that there are at least two absolutely necessary conditions for reformation. The first is that there must be an original forming. If there is no first form, there cannot possibly be a "re"-form or forming again. For anything to happen again, it must first have happened at least once. The second necessary condition for reformation is deformation. Without a deformation there is neither a need nor a possibility for reformation. Rick demonstrates the pattern clearly: formation-deformation-reformation. This is both the biblical and historical cycle.

This book puts a searchlight on biblical history's pattern of deformation—how the people of God in generation after generation turned away from the forms instituted by God. God instituted forms, but the Israelites turned them into formalism (keeping the outward forms while eclipsing the meaning and the spirit of the forms). But the prophets were not willing to throw out the forms. They did not reject the original worship patterns of God. They sought to restore them.

In our day the church is more revolutionary than reformational. By throwing out the ancient forms in an effort to be relevant and contemporary, the pattern of deformation has only been exacerbated. In this book we are escorted kindly, not rudely, back to the text of Scripture—back to the forms God established, that we may see clearly the norm for worship and Christian life. It presents the case for authentic reformation, a recovery of God's way, rather than the alluring and enticing way of this fallen world.

If Jim Boice and his co-laborers were the first wave of modern reformation, then Phillips and his generation may well push the invasion inland. God grant that it will be so.

R. C. Sproul
Orlando, Florida
Advent 2001

PREFACE

I am part of the second wave of a modern reformation. Such an assertion is bound to be subjective; yet there is a group of men and women who formed a first wave, consciously determined to pursue reformation in the evangelical church. One visible expression of this pursuit was the forming of the Alliance of Confessing Evangelicals in 1994. Under the leadership of James Montgomery Boice, with Michael S. Horton as vice chairman, this alliance gathered a number of prominent evangelicals committed to countering the church's worldly drift. In 1996 the Alliance gathered one hundred evangelical leaders for meetings at Cambridge, Massachusetts, which produced the Cambridge Declaration. That document began with what has become a rallying cry for a modern reformation:

> The Alliance of Confessing Evangelicals exists to call the church, admidst our dying culture, to repent of its worldliness, to recover and confess the truth of God's Word as did the Reformers, and to see that truth embodied in doctrine, worship and life.[1]

I was not present for these momentous events. Like many others, I first joined the modern reformation through my experience in the church. In 1990 I was attending graduate school in Philadelphia when I walked through the doors of Tenth Presbyterian Church. There I was confronted with something I had never before encountered—a real Bible preacher. To put it mildly, I was blown away. Before long I was studying my own Bible, then theology as well. My life began radically to change and my priorities to reorganize. Within a few years I had left my career and entered seminary to follow God's call to preach the Gospel.

Within a few years I was privileged to serve on the staffs of both Tenth Presbyterian Church and the Alliance of Confessing Evangelicals, becoming a colleague and friend of men I had admired for some time. As great as this honor has been, it is eclipsed by a far greater dignity, that of serving the cause of Christ and His Gospel in the church. It is this that has called me to join the second wave of the modern reformation—the conviction that reformation is the chief need in the church today and a cause worthy for the offering of my life and labor.

In military operations, it is often the first wave that achieves a beachhead, allowing the second wave to advance onward toward the objective. It is toward that end that this book is offered to the reader, with hopes that God will use what is written here to call more and more people to join the second wave of a modern reformation. This is, I believe, the great challenge of our times—that ministers and laypeople alike would take up the crusade begun by others before us, calling and leading our churches to repent of their rampant worldliness and returning them to biblical faith and practice, to the glory of God.

The material in this book first took form as seminars presented to the Philadelphia Conference on Reformation Theology over two years, 1999 and 2000. My goal, then as now, is to demonstrate the mandate for a modern reformation, as well as the pattern for such a reformation, from exclusively biblical materials. If Christians, especially Christian leaders, read this book and are caused to reflect biblically on the state of the church today, and then prayerfully to consider their role in a modern reformation, my labors will be bountifully recompensed. May Christ be lifted up in His church, and may Christians turn their faces once more to Him!

Among those deserving my thanks, the first is my wife, who patiently endured a long and weary season that was committed to the writing of this book. Her patient support and godly ministry of love is one of God's chief blessings in my life. I also wish to thank the many people associated with the Alliance of Confessing Evangelicals, both the hardworking staff and the members of the Alliance Council, headed by Michael Horton, who have extended much-valued friendship to me over many years. Among them I am especially grateful to R. C. Sproul, for his friendship and for graciously contributing his foreword. I am appreciative of Marvin Padgett and all the staff at Crossway Books for their enthusiasm for this book. As ever, I am indebted to my colleague at Tenth Presbyterian Church, Philip G. Ryken, for his godly friendship and counsel, as well as to my assistant, Patricia Russell, for innumerable helps and blessings. As with my other books, Jennifer Brewer and Bruce Bell carefully read the manuscript and made many suggestions that have improved the final product.

Finally, I thank the late James Montgomery Boice, with praise to the Lord, for his example of faith in God and in His Word. James Boice was a key statesman in the first wave of the modern reformation, and his long ministry opened the door to many advances for biblical Christianity. His fervent love for Jesus Christ and complete confidence in the Bible earned him the confidence and affection of many Christians far and wide. In his last years he often spoke of the great encouragement he gained from knowing that another wave of reformers was following after to carry on the work. I am enormously privileged to have enjoyed his personal friendship and encouragement in ministry. But above all of this, I am indebted to him for preaching God's saving Word so that this dying sinner might "take the free gift of the water of life." May God maintain James Boice's influence for the Gospel and prosper his work long after his home-going. And may our gracious Lord send fresh recruits for the reformation of His church, to the glory of God through Jesus Christ. *Soli deo gloria!*

Richard D. Phillips
Philadelphia
Reformation Day, 2001

INTRODUCTION

The terms *reformation* and *reform* have different meanings for different people. The world of criminal justice speaks of reform school as a place for errant youths. In the military, units reform after having become scattered or disorganized. Historians use the term *the Reformation* to define the momentous events of the sixteenth century that shattered the Roman Catholic hegemony in Europe and established Protestantism in its place. For many, reformation seems to mean doing things just the way the Reformers did—Luther, Calvin, or the Puritans. In the realm of theology, these terms identify a particular school of thought. *Reformed* or, more broadly, *Reformation* theology describes a system for understanding the Bible and for organizing faith and life. This system is highlighted by the "*solas*" or "alones" of the Reformation: Scripture alone, faith alone, grace alone, Christ alone, and glory to God alone (*sola scriptura, sola fide, sola gratia, solus Christus, soli deo gloria*).

The purpose of this book is to examine the theme of reformation, not merely as it refers to the sixteenth century or as it describes a particular brand of theology, but as it refers to the life of the church today. I will seek to show that reformation is a biblical concept, indeed an essential biblical mandate for every era of the Christian church. Reformation was a major concern to the prophets and apostles, and in the flow of redemptive history we will see a definite biblical pattern of reformation. It is this biblical pattern of reformation that we will particularly explore, making observations and drawing lessons for our own challenges in the church today.

GOALS OF THE BOOK

I have several goals for this study, to which I will return repeatedly. First, I want to show that reformation is not merely the pet obsession of a particular segment of the Christian church, and a narrow and cranky one at that. Many people, I find, hold this pejorative view, and not altogether without reason. But the call to reformation is not necessarily a partisan maneuver on the part of narrow conservatives. Instead, reformation is a mandate found at the core of the Bible's call to the whole community of the Christian faith, the duty that defines faithfulness in every generation of the people of God.

Second, I hope to embolden and encourage readers in the principles of reformation, which come from the Bible and not merely from Luther or Calvin or other human leaders. If what we are concerned with derives only from teachers within one tradition or lineage, then it may be good for certain circumstances and people but not normative for all times and all Christians. But if, as this book sets forth, the Scriptures themselves employ a clear pattern of fidelity versus infidelity, reformation versus deformation, then all Christians may look to these principles as a clear guide for thought and action. This is very much what we need today— not partisan pressure tactics or debates regarding mere style and preferences, but rather an analysis and framework for discussion that is demonstrably biblical and applicable to our own time. In a day where innovators are pitted against traditionalists, we urgently need a clear call for action that comes from God's Word itself. Indeed, the Reformers themselves stressed this imperative, a re-forming according to the sacred and authoritative Scriptures, and to follow their example we must do the same.

> *Reformation is a mandate found at the core of the Bible's call to the whole community of the Christian faith, the duty that defines faithfulness in every generation of the people of God.*

Third, I hope to show a definite pattern of *deformation* that occurs all through the history of God's people in Scripture. There is a pattern of disobedience and folly that is well documented in the Scriptures. Just as reformation involves a discernible pattern and flow, so also does deformation with all its terrible results. Understanding this pattern will help us to employ biblical discernment in crucial matters pressing on church leaders today. Where is the line between success and faithfulness? How are we to assess the various change and growth proposals that fly by at dizzying speed? Must we choose between a cold conservatism and a happy-clappy worldliness? While it is not my purpose to catalog the various controversies of our time, I do seek to offer principles that will form the basis for confidently biblical answers to these and other questions. Even where evangelicals are likely to disagree on matters of practice, my hope is that we might attain more agreement at the level of principle and aspiration.

IS REFORMATION A BIBLICAL IDEA?

Achieving these goals requires that we identify the biblical support for the idea of reformation. In this pursuit we will immediately encounter a linguistic matter that may confuse some people. We are concerned that we derive our thoughts from the language of the Bible, that we be constrained by the actual scriptural usage, and yet we quickly discover that the term *reformation* does not often appear in the Bible. Does this not prove that we are merely inserting our own rigid view into the interpretation of Scripture?

If you look up the noun *reformation* in your concordance, you will not be impressed by the results. In the New International Version (NIV), the word does not occur at all; in the King James Version (KJV) it occurs just once; and in the New American Standard Bible (NASB) it also is found only one time (Heb. 9:10). If you use a computerized version and you type in the verb *reform*, you will find only slightly better results. The NIV uses the word four times, all in Jeremiah and always in the form of a command. We find *reform* only once in the NASB and not at all in the KJV. By this standard *reformation* must not really be a biblical concept, or not an important one anyway. The prospects for discerning a biblical pattern seem dim at this point.

There are, however, two other words that describe what reformation is all about, and they are repeatedly encountered in the Scripture. These words are *remember* and *repent*. That is what reformation is—remembering God and His saving work and His authoritative Word, repenting *from* unfaithfulness in heart and in action and *to* the pattern God established through His Word when He formed a people for Himself. It is in the use of terms such as these that reformation occurs all through the Bible, defining faithfulness in every generation.

One of the great reformation texts is found in the opening chapters of the book of Revelation, the letters to the seven churches from the Lord

Jesus Christ. In these chapters we see our Lord, risen and exalted, standing amidst the lampstands of the church and holding the seven stars of the churches in His mighty right hand. Jesus, in this last book of God's Word, appears as the Great Reformer of His own church. That is what the seven letters He gave to John address—the reformation of what Christ Himself purchased and then formed through His servants the apostles. Ephesus was the mother church of these seven, and in the first of the letters Jesus praises this important congregation:

> *I know your works, your toil and your patient endurance, and how you cannot bear with those who are evil, but have tested those who call themselves apostles and are not, and found them to be false. I know you are enduring patiently and bearing up for my name's sake, and you have not grown weary.*
>
> —REV. 2:2-3

The next paragraph, verses 4-6, presents a well-developed definition of reformation, establishing it firmly as a mandate from the Lord:

> *But I have this against you, that you have abandoned the love you had at first. Remember therefore from where you have fallen; repent, and do the works you did at first. If not, I will come to you and remove your lampstand from its place, unless you repent.*

Reformation, as we see it biblically defined and commanded by the risen and exalted Lord Jesus Himself, consists of both holding fast to what we have received from God and the ongoing work of repenting and conforming to His Word in every area and aspect of our lives. Revelation 3:11 says, "I am coming soon. Hold fast what you have, so that no one may seize your crown." That is one side of what reformation in the church is about. The other emphasis is that of correcting or countering the impulse to deformation, repenting of the various ways in which we have turned aside or forsaken the truth. The importance of this work is not to be underestimated, at least as it is set forth by the words of our Lord. He warned His people then as He does today: "If you do not repent, I will come to you and remove your lampstand." This being the case, reformation is a matter for our closest attention and of gravest concern to the Lord.

> *Reformation consists of both holding fast to what we have received as our treasure from the Lord and engaging in the ongoing work of repenting and conforming to His Word in every area and aspect of our lives.*

THE BIBLICAL PATTERN OF REFORMATION

The idea of reformation is found not only in a few select texts, but is present in the very fabric of the biblical revelation. There is a *biblical pattern* that not only commends but demands reformation. The pattern is this: First, there is *formation* by God through the work of His prophets and apostles and in response to His mighty saving acts in history to gather a people for Himself. The two main bodies formed in Scripture are the Old Testament nation of Israel and the New Testament church. The Old and New Testaments record God's charter for each respectively. What follows, however, is sin and unfaithfulness. This is *deformation*, which is an abandonment of those commands and principles established by God in the forming of His people. Finally, in response to the presence of deformation, the Bible demands *reformation*. Formation-deformation-reformation. This is the pattern amply described in Scripture, which we will employ for our study in this book.

When we look in this way, we see that formation-deformation-reformation is found in the Bible with major structural significance. Anyone familiar with Old Testament history will immediately recognize this. In the days of Moses, God *formed* His people as the nation Israel. He established principles and rules that were to govern that formation. The book of Deuteronomy is the key document detailing this formation and the principles involved. Practically all the rest of Old Testament history provides the record of *deformation* as the people of God rebelled and forsook Him in one way or another. Along the way there were lesser and greater attempts at *reformation*. This, for instance, was the main agenda of the prophets. The prophets were the great reformers of the Old Testament according to God's own description. We see this in the book of Jeremiah, who was the last of that long and great line of prophets before cataclysmic judgment in the fall of Jerusalem and the Babylonian captivity. Here was God's summary of the whole prophetic mission as one of reformation:

Again and again I sent all my servants the prophets to you. They said, "Each of you must turn from your wicked ways and reform your actions; do not follow other gods to serve them. Then you will live in the land I have given to you and your fathers."

—JER. 35:15, NIV, emphasis added

I have pointed out that the term *reform* is seldom found in the text of Scripture, although its constituent parts of *remember* and *repent* are commonly found. It is worth pointing out, however, that when the word *reform* does occur, as in this passage, it is used as a summary description for the whole work of all the prophets. This is what is going on in the books describing Israel's life from the time of Moses to God's judgment in the destruction of the city and its temple. Israel's rejection of the prophetic call to reformation—to remember and repent—anticipated God's judgment on the deformed nation, a judgment that came to a head in the Babylonian conquest and captivity.

In the days of Moses, God formed His people as the nation Israel. Practically all the rest of Old Testament history is the record of deformation as the people of God rebelled and forsook Him. Along the way there were attempts at reformation, which was the main agenda of the prophets.

Even after this terrible judgment, reformation is what we see going on in the pages of the Old Testament. God's deliverance of Israel in the time of Ezra and Nehemiah was a classic example of reformation. It was a reformation performed by God through His servants, with a fresh application of the principles and commands seen in the original formation under Moses.

This biblical pattern provides the outline we will follow in this book. First, we will examine the pattern of *formation* as it plays out in the Old Testament. This begins with an examination of the principles embodied in the book of Deuteronomy, which more than any other document served as the charter for God's formation of Israel as a nation. Second, we will see how through the centuries Israel betrayed these principles and *deformed* what God had established. Then we will observe *reformation* in action through such great biblical figures as Jehoshaphat and Josiah.

Our study will conclude with an examination of this same pattern in the New Testament and the apostolic church. In particular, we will focus on the reforming efforts of the apostle Paul with regard to the Galatian churches. Finally we will compare all that we have found with the seven letters to the churches that appear in Revelation 2—3, given through the apostle John by the risen and exalted Jesus Himself, the Great Reformer, who stands amidst the candlesticks as Lord of the Church.

THOU MAY'ST SMILE

Before concluding this introduction, I want to offer some perspective on the situation in the church today and the pressing need for reformation that we find before us. It seems to me that there are two errors into which we may fall. On the one hand many discount talk of trouble and the need for reform as alarmist and unduly negative. On the other hand, others withdraw in despair over the singularly wretched conditions of our day. But what we are going through today, as so many churches are wandering from biblical principles—both in terms of the means they employ and the ends they are seeking—is not something strange or unique. This is a vital thing for us to understand. On the contrary, it is the normal experience of the church. Among the truths our study will show is that deformation is not something strange or unusual, but is a recurring phenomenon we should expect, watch out for, and respond to with awareness and resolve, but not with surprise or dismay.

The apostle Peter wrote in his first epistle, "Beloved, do not be surprised at the fiery trial when it comes upon you to test you, as though something strange were happening to you" (4:12). We might adopt that language and say, "Beloved, do not be surprised at the woeful state of the church and the urgent need for reformation, as though something strange were happening." One way or another, every generation encounters deviation from the pattern set down in Scripture, and every generation has to combat deformation with biblical reformation.

The more Christian literature I read, the more I am convinced that however bleak things may appear today—and surely they do—ours is not the only troubled time in the church. In an essay given by Martyn Lloyd-Jones a mere generation ago, the great preacher articulated his conclusion that the evangelical church had retreated to roughly the same position as Roman Catholicism before the Reformation. That was the sober assessment a generation ago, and our vast biblical illiteracy confirms it today.[1] If you go back a little further than Lloyd-Jones, to the end of the nineteenth century, you find the great Anglican bishop J. C. Ryle writing about the terrible state of affairs in his time with words that could also be applied to our own:

> We have hundreds of ministers, both inside and outside the Church of England, who seem not to have a single bone in their body of divinity. They have no definite opinions; they belong to no school or party; they are so afraid of 'extreme views,' that they have no views at all. . . . And last, and worst of all, we have myriads of worshippers, respectable church-going people, who have no distinct and definite views about any point of theology. . . . They are 'tossed to and fro, like children, by every wind of doctrine;' often carried away by some new excitement and sensational movement; ever ready for new things, because they have no firm grasp on the old; and utterly unable to 'render a reason of the hope that is in them.'[2]

That was written in 1881, but if it were published today we would find ourselves in agreement. If you go back a generation earlier than that you find Charles Haddon Spurgeon saying this:

> This age is a doubting age. It swarms with doubters as Egypt of old with frogs. You rub against them everywhere. Everybody is doubting everything, not merely in religion, but in politics and social economics, in everything indeed. . . . Well, brethren, as the age is doubting, it is wise for us to put our foot down and stand still where we are sure we have truth beneath us.[3]

In generation after generation, as you go back you find the same thing. There is therefore a constant need for and a tradition of reformation that stretches back to the great Reformers, and back before them to the early church and the apostolic age itself. The point is this: Let us not be discouraged or alarmed by the great need for reformation in our day, but rather let us show the kind of bold resolve of those "children of Issachar," described in 1 Chronicles 12:32 as "men who had understanding of the times, to know what Israel ought to do."

To achieve this we first of all must understand the Bible, where reformation is set forth as a constant need and a serious challenge of faith. But it is also a privilege for those who wish to serve our Lord Jesus Christ in the age in which we are found, and it comes with great promises that should make us confident of God's blessing, particularly as we put our trust in His mighty, saving Word.

This book was written with praise to God for the life and ministry of the late Dr. James Montgomery Boice, a great preacher of the Gospel and a true reformer, who encouraged me greatly in this work as it was originally presented in seminar form. James Boice was saddened and disturbed by the trends developing in the church during his lifetime, and he often spoke sobering and challenging words on the topic of faithfulness to Christ. None of this, however, took from him the great joy of his salvation and a soaring confidence in God's triumph through His Word. I recall many times standing next to his lively frame as he sang with gusto, uninhibited in his glee, especially when it was a hymn celebrating the sufficiency of our God and the believer's unshakable hope in Jesus Christ. One such hymn, written by John Newton, encourages every servant of God in the joy that comes from our salvation. On the basis of these scriptural truths, let us turn earnestly to our task, but not without the hope and assurance that belong to us in Jesus Christ.

> *Glorious things of thee are spoken, Zion, city of our God;*
> *He whose word cannot be broken formed thee for his own abode:*
> *On the Rock of Ages founded, what can shake thy sure repose?*
> *With salvation's walls surrounded, thou may'st smile at all thy*
> *foes.*

PART ONE

FORMATION AND DEFORMATION IN OLD TESTAMENT ISRAEL

1

ON THE PLAINS OF MOAB:
ISRAEL IN FORMATION

Deuteronomy means "second law" (*deutero-nomos*), and the name signifies the setting in which the book was given. Its opening verses tell us that its message was given through Moses forty years after the Israelites' departure from Egypt in the Exodus, on the plains of Moab across the Jordan River from the Land of Promise. In terms of sheer drama, there are few scenes that can match this one.

For one thing, this marked the final public act of Moses' illustrious career. Everything in his life, from his birth with its providential protection to the meeting with God at the burning bush, from the mighty confrontations with Pharaoh and the stunning passage through the Red Sea to the receiving of the Ten Commandments from the very finger of God on Mount Sinai, had pointed to and led up to this moment. The aim of it all was the establishment of Israel as God's nation in Canaan, in fulfillment of God's promise to Abraham so long before. In a very real sense, Deuteronomy witnesses Moses setting in place what his entire career had sought and served.

Equally dramatic were the recipients of this book, the second generation of the Israel of the Exodus. Where was the first generation? They had died, their bones littering the desert wastes between Egypt and Canaan. Despite all they had seen and received in God's mighty acts of deliverance, they had not put their trust in Him, and God judged them in response. As the writer of Hebrews would later observe in the New Testament: "For who were those who heard and yet rebelled? Was it not all those who left Egypt led by Moses? And with whom was he provoked for forty years? Was it not with those who sinned, whose bodies fell in the wilderness?" (3:16-17). That generation had spurned the promises; so here was assembled the second generation as God confronted them with the same mandate. Here Israel would receive again God's Law, with His commandments for their life together as a people. This was not a casual gathering, but one fraught with sober decision.

The spectacle itself must have been amazing to behold. Here stood the entire second generation of Israel after the great events of the Exodus, numbered in the hundreds of thousands, stretched out by family and clan and tribe upon the plains of Moab. The book of Numbers tells us that over 600,000 adult male Israelites had begun the journey from Egypt, not counting the women or the children. Here in the book of Deuteronomy is the generation of their children, surely a vast host. Before them is the Land of Promise, the land their fathers were too fearful and disbelieving to enter, the land Moses himself could only gaze upon from afar, not being permitted by God to set his foot upon its sacred soil. This gathering would be his last public act before climbing up Mount Nebo to cast his gaze upon the land God had promised to Abraham, to which he had himself been leading Israel these many decades. Deuteronomy 1:5 tersely sets the stage: "East of the Jordan in the territory of Moab, Moses began to expound this law" (NIV).

DEUTERONOMY AS THE BOOK OF FORMATION

The book of Deuteronomy records this decisive moment when Israel transitioned from the Exodus to the Promised Land. Christopher Wright elaborates, "Geographically, historically, and theologically, Deuteronomy is a book 'on the boundary.'" As such it serves as a key resource from God for those seeking divine guidance as they go forward into a new situation. Wright adds that Deuteronomy speaks "powerfully through the ages to every generation of God's people called to move across the ever shifting boundary from past experience of God into future unknown circumstances."[1] Deuteronomy served as a charter for Israel's life in the Promised Land, and thus Moses gathered the twelve tribes to reconfirm their covenant with the Lord. Here the Law was reasserted and reapplied, and the covenant was renewed with this next generation, the generation that under Joshua would actually enter into and seize the territory ahead. It is called the Second Law not because it differs from the first, but because it is God's formative Law reasserted and reapplied. It comes in the second phase of the Exodus, not as Israel escapes from the land of bondage, but as they are established in a home as the holy nation of the living God.

So important is the book of Deuteronomy that an enormous amount of scholarly ink has been devoted to it. This book of the Bible has great significance, for what was set forth here served as the normative charter for all that Israel would do in the years ahead. Deuteronomy was to Israel what the Constitution is to the United States of America. Hence, much of the rest of the Old Testament looks back to Deuteronomy in an explicit way. It is rightly said that the books of Joshua and Judges, Samuel and Kings and Chronicles (which together are often called the Deuteronomic History) tell the ongoing story of Israel as sermons preached from the text of Deuteronomy. In a very special sense Deuteronomy was *the* Word of God by which the rest of the Old Testament was bound. This does not discount the vital significance of the rest of the Torah—Genesis, Exodus, Leviticus, and Numbers—but rather sets forth the distinct historical and theological significance of this formative book of the Old Testament witness.

> *Deuteronomy was to Israel what the Constitution is to the United States of America. In a very special sense Deuteronomy was the Word of God by which the rest of the Old Testament was bound.*

Deuteronomy is important to our examination of the Bible's pattern of reformation because it marks an explicit starting point. The Pentateuch as a whole may be said to articulate the formative principles for God's people, and yet in Deuteronomy we have a distinct summary and application of the whole, given at an identifiable moment of formation. Certainly the later writers of the Old Testament saw it this way, often citing it as the definitive norm. Jesus held it in like esteem; when tempted by Satan in the desert, He drew all three of his biblical responses from the book of Deuteronomy.

Deuteronomy is filled with instructions, rules, and commands, as even a cursory reading will uncover. At its heart, however, is the covenant between the Lord and His people. A biblical covenant is a relationship established and administered by God according to His will. The covenant relationship most familiar to us today is marriage, and indeed this very description is given for the covenant God established with Israel and reaffirmed through Moses on the plains of Moab. Later, when the Israelites broke the covenant, Jeremiah would complain on God's behalf, "I gave faithless Israel her certificate of divorce and sent her away because of all her adulteries" (Jer. 3:8, NIV).

Due to its vast amount of material, Deuteronomy is not easily summarized, and scholars have employed a great many approaches for organizing its material. However, the principles given to God's people, mandates to define their faithfulness to Him at this crucial formative period, are clearly set forth in this book of Scripture. I want to highlight five distinct themes or principles that can be easily established from the book of Deuteronomy: 1) exclusive and heartfelt devotion to the Lord; 2) holiness before the world; 3) salvation by grace alone; 4) the normative and binding character of prior revelation; and 5) the necessity of social justice and mercy. The remainder of this chapter will examine these principles.

EXCLUSIVE AND HEARTFELT DEVOTION TO THE LORD

At the very heart of Deuteronomy's message is the claim that "the LORD" (Yahweh) alone is God and that He alone has claim on the hearts of His people. This is *the* great principle of Deuteronomy, *the* principle governing the formation of the people of God.

The great passage that identifies this principle as the heart of the covenant relationship is Deuteronomy 6:4-9, which includes the verse Jesus Himself described as the greatest and therefore focal commandment of the entire Law. Even today the halls of synagogues resound with these words that more than any other have focused the identity of the Jewish people. The passage begins with what is known as the *Shema*, the Hebrew word for the command, "Hear."

> *"Hear, O Israel: The LORD our God, the LORD is one. You shall love the LORD your God with all your heart and with all your soul and with all your might. And these words that I command you today shall be on your heart. You shall teach them diligently to your children, and shall talk of them when you sit in your house, and when you walk by the way, and when you lie down,*

*and when you rise. You shall bind them as a sign on your hand,
and they shall be as frontlets between your eyes. You shall write
them on the doorposts of your house and on your gates.*

—DEUT. 6:4-9

Here is the heart of the covenant, given at the forming of the
nation Israel: exclusive covenant love between the Lord and His people. "God has shown His love to you"—that is what the Exodus
revealed; "now love Him with all your heart and soul and strength, in
this generation and in all that will follow." Israel's love for God was
to find intense expression through obedience to His commands, a love
for what He had done and taught, so that these things above all others would shape and form and perpetuate this society of the people of
God. As the Lord is "one," so the people's love for Him was to flow
from the wholeness of each person and of the society of His people.
Verses 8-9 speak metaphorically regarding how deeply this command
was to shape their lives, words that some present-day Jews have
sought to literally obey with scroll-boxes tied to their heads and
hands. What God really desired was that the message be emblazoned
inwardly and spiritually: His commands to love and serve Him only
were "to be on your heart" (v. 6).

An essential feature of the love God desired was its *exclusivity*. The
covenant established a marriage relationship. Describing the whole
Exodus, including the formation of the people in Deuteronomy,
Jeremiah would later write, "I took them by the hand to bring them out
of the land of Egypt. . . . I was their husband" (Jer. 31:32). From God's
point of view, His covenant with Israel was a marriage; He gave Himself
to Israel, His bride, and expected exclusive love in return. Later, when
God judged the idolatrous nation, the blame for breaking the covenant
fell squarely on them, for God had redeemed and married Israel in mar-
velous grace.

Another feature of this love was its source. It began with and was
based not upon the people's love for God but on His love for them. As
the apostle John would later explain to Christians, "Not that we have
loved God but that he loved us" (1 John 4:10). This is the point of
Deuteronomy 4:32-34, where Moses recounts the marvel of God's love
for Israel, pointing to the Exodus as a remarkable instance of divine
salvation:

*For ask now of the days that are past, which were before you,
since the day that God created man on the earth, and ask from
one end of heaven to the other, whether such a great thing as this
has ever happened or was ever heard of. Did any people ever hear
the voice of a god speaking out of the midst of the fire, as you have
heard, and still live? Or has any god ever attempted to go and take
a nation for himself from the midst of another nation, by trials,
by signs, by wonders, and by war, by a mighty hand and an outstretched arm, and by great deeds of terror, all of which the* LORD
your God did for you in Egypt before your eyes?

What was the point of these great demonstrations of power and
love? Verse 35 drives the point home: "To you it was shown, that you
might know that the Lord is God; *there is no other besides him*" (ital-
ics mine). God had saved them with a singular love; in response they
were to own and worship only Him as God.

The Lord alone is the God of His people. The Exodus salvation
intended to teach and reveal this great principle. To Him and Him alone
were His people to give their hearts and their minds, their souls and their
strength. As Christopher Wright explains, Israel's monotheistic passion
for the one God "was not the conclusion of an evolution of religious
speculation, but an assertion generated out of historical experience and
grounded there."[2]

---

*The Lord alone is the God of His people. The Exodus salva-
tion was intended to teach and reveal this great principle. To
Him and Him alone were His people to give their hearts and
their minds, their souls and their strength.*

This principle had vital implications for the future leadership of
Israel. Instead of a king, Moses set over Israel elders and judges who
would lead in plurality. In Deuteronomy 1 Moses explains: "So I took
the heads of your tribes, wise and experienced men, and set them as
heads over you, commanders of thousands, commanders of hundreds,
commanders of fifties, commanders of tens, and officers, throughout
your tribes. And I charged your judges at that time, 'Hear the cases
between your brothers, and judge righteously between a man and his
brother. . . . You shall not be partial in judgment. You shall hear the small

and the great alike. You shall not be intimidated by anyone, for the judgment is God's'" (vv. 15-17). Israel did in fact have a king—it was the Lord Himself who ruled through the elders and judges and prophets. This comes through clearly in Moses' final blessing of the people, which began with praise to God: "He said, 'The LORD came from Sinai . . . he came from the ten thousands of holy ones, with flaming fire at his right hand. Yes, he loved his people . . . so they followed in your steps, receiving direction from you" (Deut. 33:2-3). Of the Lord, Moses concludes, "Thus the LORD became king in Jeshurun, when the heads of the people were gathered, all the tribes of Israel together" (v. 5). God Himself was king over His people, with qualified officers governing in His name. Therefore the homage, allegiance, and devotion commonly due to kings was reserved for Him alone among the people of Israel.

Deuteronomy makes clear that teaching and doctrine were essential to the people's love relationship with the Lord. Israel was to sustain its devotion on the knowledge of what the Lord had done as deliverer and faithful husband. Their love was to consist of exclusive devotion to the Lord, based on a doctrinal commitment that first moved the heart and then manifested itself in practical conformity to God's commands. Consider, for instance, another of Moses' summary statements, this time in Deuteronomy 10:12-13:

> *And now, Israel, what does the LORD your God require of you, but to fear the LORD your God, to walk in all his ways, to love him, to serve the LORD your God with all your heart and with all your soul, and to keep the commandments and statutes of the LORD, which I am commanding you today for your good?*

Note the interplay between the heart and the hands, the inseparable link between the inward and the outward: Fear—walk; love—serve and observe "with all your heart and with all your soul." Moses concludes the passage with this famous and vitally significant statement: "Circumcise therefore the foreskin of your heart, and be no longer stubborn" (v. 16).

It is sometimes said that in the Sermon on the Mount Jesus gave the spiritual meaning of the Law that was missing in the Old Testament. But this is not true. The Law was never intended as a merely external code of simple behavior. Always, the relationship between God and His people was to be one of heart devotion and love.

This is the first principle of formation in the book of Deuteronomy: exclusive and heartfelt love to the Lord. This mandate was theologically centered—it was based upon who God is; it was doctrinally determined—that is, it focused on the people's knowledge and understanding of God's saving acts in history; and it was expressed through wholehearted lifestyle worship. Israel's response to Yahweh was to be intensely theological and doctrinal, and with an equal intensity it was to be practical in its manifestation in life.

HOLINESS OR SEPARATION

The first principle detailed the vertical dimension—Israel's relationship to the Lord versus all other claimants to worship. The second principle acted horizontally—the command to holiness, that is, separation *to* God and *from* the world. This comes through in Deuteronomy 28:9-10:

> *The LORD will establish you as a people holy to himself, as he has sworn to you, if you keep the commandments of the LORD your God and walk in his ways. And all the peoples of the earth shall see that you are called by the name of the LORD, and they shall be afraid of you.*

Deuteronomy 14:2 adds, "For you are a people holy to the LORD your God, and the LORD has chosen you to be a people for his treasured possession, out of all the peoples who are on the face of the earth."

Israel was to be different—purposefully different—from all other peoples. They were not to copy the ways of the nations around them or the people living in the land they would soon occupy. They were to be a holy nation in the world, like the ark on the flooding seas, revealing to the nations the only true God and salvation. To do this they had to be different. They were not to marry other peoples or live with them, much less to learn methods of worship from them: "For these nations, which you are about to dispossess, listen to fortune-tellers and to diviners. But as for you, the LORD your God has not allowed you to do this" (Deut. 18:14).

What we see in effect is a centripetal principle. Webster's definition of centripetal force is this: "acting in a direction toward a center or axis."[3] Israel was to be directed inward, not outward; the pull was to be toward the center. Yahweh was found there, where the Ark of the Covenant camped in the center of the twelve tribes. Therefore the force was to be centripetal (inward—toward the Lord and His commands) and not centrifugal (outward—toward the nations and their ways).

> *You shall not worship the* LORD *your God in that way, for every abominable thing that the* LORD *hates they have done for their gods, for they even burn their sons and their daughters in the fire to their gods. . . . You are the sons of the* LORD *your God. . . . For you are a people holy to the* LORD *your God, and the* LORD *has chosen you to be a people for his treasured possession, out of all the peoples who are on the face of the earth.*
> —DEUT. 12:31; 14:1-2

God's people were to be visibly, discernibly different from those who were not His people, and this difference was to be manifested in their practices, in what they did and how they did it. This was one of the functions of the Levitical restrictions on food and clothing and hairstyle—the intent was to segregate God's people from those outside. Otherwise they would be sure to experience pollution and be led astray. So their *practice* was to be different, their *logic* different, their *intent* different, their *goals* different, their *methods* different from all those around them, lest they should forsake the Lord and be abandoned by Him in return.

> *God's people were to be visibly different, and this difference was to be manifested in their practices, in what they did and how they did it. They were not to marry other peoples or live with them, much less to learn methods of worship from them.*

SALVATION BY GRACE ALONE

A third principle clearly expressed in Deuteronomy is: *salvation is by grace alone.* A famous statement of this occurs in 7:7-8:

> *It was not because you were more in number than any other people that the* LORD *set his love on you and chose you, for you were the fewest of all peoples, but it is because the* LORD *loves*

you and is keeping the oath that he swore to your fathers, that the LORD has brought you out with a mighty hand and redeemed you from the house of slavery, from the hand of Pharaoh king of Egypt.

Israel was elected by God's sovereign grace; the explanation for their salvation was found in Him and not in them. How lovely the Lord puts this, that while they had nothing to commend themselves, He "set his love" on the people, and on this unexplained grace they were to set their hopes and confidence.

God considered this teaching so important that in Deuteronomy 27 we read of provisions He made for it to be taught in a living drama involving the entire nation. When Israel entered Canaan they were to form themselves on two mountains, Mount Gerizim and Mount Ebal. Half the tribes would form on Mount Gerizim and cry out, "Blessed are those who obey God's commands." Then they would call out all the commands and all the blessings for obedience. The other half stood on Mount Ebal and cried, "Cursed is he who breaks God's commands, who rebels and disobeys," then recited all the commands and all the curses for disobedience. What is so telling is that they were then to set up the altar to worship the Lord. But on which mountain would it be erected? Would it be on Mount Gerizim, where joyful voices extolled the virtues of obedience? Or would it be on Mount Ebal, where mournful hearts reflected on the weighty curse of sin? Deuteronomy 27:4-7 tells us the altar would be installed not on Mount Gerizim, not on the ground of their own obedience and achievement, but on Mount Ebal. They were to worship the Lord in the context of their failure and not of their success, in the context of their transgression and not of their obedience to God's holy Law.

And when you have crossed over the Jordan, you shall set up these stones, concerning which I command you today, on Mount Ebal, and you shall plaster them with plaster. And there you shall build an altar to the LORD your God, an altar of stones. You shall wield no iron tool on them; you shall build an altar to the LORD your God of uncut stones. And you shall offer burnt offerings on it to the LORD your God, and you shall sacrifice peace offerings and shall eat there, and you shall rejoice before the LORD your God.

Note that the altar was to be unblemished by human works, while they worshiped on the basis of a divinely provided sacrifice in the context of human failure.

This teaching of salvation by grace alone constrained their attitude toward salvation: They were not to trust their own works but only God's grace. They were to worship by a blood sacrifice that signified the atonement God would provide. But salvation by grace alone not only constrained their worship—it also offered God's people a wonderful assurance and joy. Because of God's grace, the Israelites were not to fear the superior armies of those around them but were to trust Him and beseech Him and turn their hearts to Him, for the Lord would be their salvation in battle. The faithful God who had saved them not because of their merit but because of His own love could be relied upon to hear their cry. Salvation by grace alone was also to shape their life together as a community of grace, to determine even their politics and military strategy. Israel was not to seek success or safety or blessing through human means or strength, but through a reliance on divine power and mercy. When enemies drew near, it was on His grace that they were to take their stand:

> *Do not fear or panic or be in dread of them, for the LORD your God is he who goes with you to fight for you against your enemies, to give you the victory.*
>
> —DEUT. 20:3-4

The altar was to be unblemished by human works. They worshiped on the basis of a divinely provided sacrifice in the context of human failure.

THE NORMATIVE CHARACTER OF PRIOR REVELATION

The fourth principle is one that would become particularly relevant in later years. In Deuteronomy 18 it is articulated in the context of a promise—namely, that the Lord would send others like Moses to bear His revelation to the people. The natural question that accompanied this, however, was how the people were to tell a true prophet from a false one. That this posed a real danger is apparent from what God said to Moses:

I will raise up for them a prophet like you from among their
brothers. And I will put my words in his mouth, and he shall
speak to them all that I command him. And whoever will not
listen to my words that he shall speak in my name, I myself
will require it of him. But the prophet who presumes to speak
a word in my name that I have not commanded him to speak,
or who speaks in the name of other gods, that same prophet
shall die.

—VV. 18-20

A principle was therefore needed for testing a supposed prophet. Prophets claimed to speak for God, and so there had to be a means of testing those who made such a claim. The principle God gave was this: God will send prophets, indeed one Great Prophet is coming, and while you are obliged to follow them, you are also required not to follow any impostors. How, then, are you to tell the difference? Is it the ability to predict the future that defines a true prophet? What about signs and miracles? These things were indeed indicators of a prophet, and yet they were not enough. It was conceivable that false prophets could engage in at least the appearance of supernatural power and prediction. A prophet's authority would be ultimately determined in that he spoke what God had commanded. The key idea is that prior revelation was binding and normative with regard to new claims to revelation. This comes out particularly clearly in Deuteronomy 13:1-5:

If a prophet or a dreamer of dreams arises among you and gives
you a sign or a wonder, and the sign or wonder that he tells you
comes to pass, and if he says, "Let us go after other gods,"
which you have not known, and "let us serve them," you shall
not listen to the words of that prophet or that dreamer of
dreams. For the LORD your God is testing you, to know
whether you love the LORD your God with all your heart and
with all your soul. You shall walk after the LORD your God and
fear him and keep his commandments and obey his voice, and
you shall serve him and hold fast to him. But that prophet or
that dreamer of dreams shall be put to death, because he has
taught rebellion against the LORD your God.

Once Israel had received clear revelation from God, that revelation was determinative for all that would follow. The one thing the people could be sure of was that God would not contradict Himself. God's unchanging character was sure, while alleged miraculous signs and prophecies were not. God's revealed Word had primacy over all other considerations when deciding whether to follow a purported holy man; even with all the other evidence stacked against it, the people were to hold to God's Word. We can see, then, why Jesus insisted, in the Sermon on the Mount, "Do not think that I have come to abolish the Law or the Prophets; I have not come to abolish them but to fulfill them" (Matt. 5:17). Otherwise He would have disqualified himself under the provisions of Israel's charter and could not have been the Great Prophet come to fulfill all that was written before Him. No new prophet could contradict an older prophet; truth that God had revealed brought continuity and binding authority into the future.

Once Israel had received clear revelation from God, that revelation was determinative for all that followed.

THE NECESSITY OF SOCIAL JUSTICE AND MERCY

Finally, Deuteronomy betrays a distinct concern for social justice and mercy. Israelites were not to use phony weights for measuring, and they were not to move boundary stones. This principle is closely related to other principles and flows out from them, particularly the call to holiness and the principle of grace. Here are some examples from Deuteronomy:

> *If among you, one of your brothers should become poor, in any of your towns within your land that the LORD your God is giving you, you shall not harden your heart or shut your hand against your poor brother, but you shall open your hand to him and lend him sufficient for his need, whatever it may be.*
> —15:7-8

> *When you beat your olive trees, you shall not go over them again. It shall be for the sojourner, the fatherless, and the widow. When you gather the grapes of your vineyard, you shall not strip it afterward. It shall be for the sojourner, the father-*

less, and the widow. You shall remember that you were a slave
in the land of Egypt; therefore I command you to do this.

—24:20-22

This chapter has not attempted to provide a comprehensive survey of the vitally important book of Deuteronomy, the formative charter for the Old Testament people and a book with serious implications for New Testament believers. But this was an important starting point and, as we will see, is an effective baseline for considering later deformation and reformation. Deformation would arise when Israel forgot or betrayed these God-given commands; similarly, no reformation is biblically complete unless these foundational principles are reestablished in the life of God's people. The principles articulated here should be familiar to every Christian, for they ring throughout the New Testament as well. With these principles, Israel was formed by God and was chartered as His own nation in the land of promise. This was *formation*. In almost all the rest of the Old Testament, in nearly all the history from that time forward, we see the sad and sordid record of *deformation*. To this we now turn our attention.

2

"Give Us a King!"

We have seen Deuteronomy as a covenant-making book, the charter for the nation of God's people who soon would be established across the Jordan. Deuteronomy also contains a good deal of prophecy, mainly foretelling the deformation that would come and the calamities that would be its result. The book predicts a horrible catalog of disasters that would fall upon Israel, caused by the people's disobedience. As we see the unfolding of this pattern of rebellion and apostasy and subsequent judgment—what I am calling deformation—we learn from the Bible not only *what* took place but *why*, not only the *effects* but also the *causes*. It is in this manner that this record presents valuable lessons to our own age with regard to a biblical perspective on means and ends.

AN OMINOUS PRELUDE

In our last chapter we saw the instructions God gave to the tribes regarding the blessings and curses of His Law. Half of the people were to stand on Mount Gerizim to recite blessings that would follow obedience, the other half on Mount Ebal calling forth the curses upon disobedience. This was not a passing moment in the ritual of Israel. Here was a gathering in the Promised Land under Joshua that was conjoined to the one in Moab under Moses recorded in Deuteronomy. Here the terms for the future of the nation were set down. In the case of either a future obedience and blessing or a future disobedience and curse, the lines were drawn back in time to this covenant ceremony and its clearly defined terms.

The book of Deuteronomy does not give equal space to both options. In reading Moses' instructions in Deuteronomy 27, we find a cursory treatment of the blessings (verses 1-14), but a detailed drum roll as the curses spew forth (verses 15-26). First come the blessings on obedience; in fourteen verses in Deuteronomy 28 he gives a lovely statement of what life will be like in an obedient and godly nation: "Blessed shall be the fruit of your womb and the fruit of your ground and the fruit of your cattle. . . . Blessed shall be your basket and your kneading bowl. Blessed shall you be when you come in, and blessed shall you be when you go out" (verses 4-6). A clear and wonderful future stretched out before the feet of Israel; we are reminded of Adam and Eve before the two trees in the Garden, the fullness of blessing within such easy reach.

Verse 15 begins the warning against disobedience: "But if you will not obey the voice of the LORD your God or be careful to do all his commandments and his statutes that I command you today, then all these curses shall come upon you and overtake you." Next comes a litany deliberately shaped to mirror that of the blessings: "Cursed shall you be in the city, and cursed shall you be in the field. Cursed shall be your basket and your kneading bowl. Cursed shall be the fruit of your womb. . . . Cursed shall you be when you come in, and cursed shall you be when you go out" (vv. 16-19). So far, all of this is perfectly consistent with what we would expect. The Lord, like earthly lords who made treaties and agreements with their vassals, could be expected to lay out stipulations with blessings and curses for obedience or disobedience. Israel already had the blessings laid before them—by grace and not by works; yet the Lord made clear the results of infidelity to His gracious and sovereign rule. As Christopher Wright observes, "Blessing . . . is there to be enjoyed, but can be enjoyed only by living in God's way in the land God is giving them."[1]

This is the question with which Israel begins its life in the land, a question that is renewed in every generation of God's people: Which way will they go—obedience or infidelity? In the rest of Deuteronomy 28, we get a sense that Israel was going to follow in the path of our first parents, insanely choosing what was forbidden and thus being cast outside the sphere of God's rich blessing. Following the fourteen verses in which Moses spells out the joys of obedience are fifty-four verses that progressively move from a sense of what *might be* to what *will be*. Both blessing and curse are equally *possible*, but in this account they do not seem equally *likely*.

Commentators give a variety of reasons for the preponderance of attention given to the curses in comparison to the blessings. Perhaps it is because a sovereign lord inevitably places more weight on threat than enticement, the same way parents do with children staying home with a baby-sitter for the first time. Such is the sinful nature of man that God needs to spend more time on the consequences of sin than those of obedience. According to another view, God stresses the coming difficulty because it is only in trials that sinful people learn to rely upon the Lord. Another view holds that since God's judgments will be so severe, the clearest of warnings needed to be given. This way, in the event of judgment the people would realize that the fault lay in their own rather than God's unfaithfulness. In the case of future judgment, Raymond Brown writes, "The word they had ignored in their prosperity would become eloquent in their grief."[2]

This long section of curses may be read at leisure, though surely not with ease. They include confusion and ruin of every sort, economic calamity and military collapse, periods of long despair and sudden bursts of great destruction. In reading this ongoing stream of judgment, the modern reader cannot fail to see the fall of Samaria in 722 B.C., the siege of Jerusalem that ended in 586 B.C., and even the destruction of Jerusalem in A.D. 70, complete with the horrors of plague and cannibalism. "All these curses shall come upon you," Moses warned, "because you did not serve the LORD your God with joyfulness and gladness of heart, because of the abundance of all things" (vv. 45, 47). Peter Craigie sums up in a manner that reflects the impression we get today: "When the substance of Deut. 28:15-68 is read with a knowledge of the subsequent history of Israel as a nation, the curses seem to assume an awful inevitability." All of this might truly be avoided, and yet a people already bearing the curse of sin must inexorably gravitate in that direction. "When it is recalled further that the Israelites were not an exceptional people, but reflected in their perversity the nature of sinful man, then the inevitability of the curse weighs equally on the modern reader."[3] We in the church today are thus reminded that all our methods and strategies must contend with the same grim reality concerning human nature. More than that, we are reminded of the only remedy for our dread condition—namely, God's gift of His own Son to die on the cross, who in that way "redeemed us from the curse of the law by becoming a curse for us" (Gal. 3:13).

A people already bearing the curse of sin must inexorably gravitate in that direction. All our methods and strategies today must contend with the same grim reality concerning human nature.

THE DEUTERONOMIC HISTORY

The history of Israel from its entry into Canaan until its exile from the land over seven hundred years later is varied and complex. Despite the ominous warnings given by Moses, the story begins gloriously. In many ways the book of Joshua is the high-water mark of the Old Testament; here we see what can be if the people turn their hearts to the Lord, quickly and readily repent of their sins, and live by faith in the light of God's grace.

The book of Joshua begins what is called the Deuteronomic History—that is, the biblical record of Israel from its entry into Canaan to the Babylonian exile, all based upon the formative charter of the book of Deuteronomy. This history includes the books of Judges, 1 and 2 Samuel, and 1 and 2 Kings, which together tell over seven centuries of Israel's story, from the heydays of Joshua to the ignominious destruction of Jerusalem under the last of the kings. It is a history that tumbles more or less downhill from the triumphs of Joshua. Compared to that beginning, even the triumphant career of King David, recounted in 1 and 2 Samuel, operates on a much lower altitude. It is a bad sign when a people's best days are its first.

The period after Joshua is recorded in the book of Judges. Here was a lengthy period of disarray and disobedience, with the subsequent result of judgment from God. Judges ominously picks up the account left off by Joshua with these words:

> *And the people served the LORD all the days of Joshua, and all the days of the elders who outlived Joshua, who had seen all the great work that the LORD had done for Israel. . . . And all that generation also were gathered to their fathers. And there arose another generation after them who did not know the LORD or the work that he had done for Israel. And the people of Israel did what was evil in the sight of the LORD and served the Baals. And they abandoned the LORD, the God of their fathers, who*

had brought them out of the land of Egypt. They went after other gods, from among the gods of the peoples who were around them, and bowed down to them. And they provoked the LORD *to anger. They abandoned the* LORD *and served the Baals and the Ashtaroth.*

—JUDG. 2:7-13

The age of the judges witnesses the trampling of nearly every principle and command set forth in Deuteronomy by the unbelieving people. Here in this book we find deformation on a grand scale, with the predictable response of judgment from the Lord, just as Deuteronomy had set forth. It is amazing that God did not reject the people altogether, and yet this period ends with hope from God in the person of Samuel.

Samuel was one of the great transitional figures of the Bible, one who served as both prophet and judge. Samuel was a great reformer, restoring faithfulness to the Lord and receiving God's blessing in both victory and peace. Accordingly, the end of Samuel's life was a pivotal time, another occasion when two different paths stretched before the nation, just as when Joshua prepared to die and spoke his memorable and challenging words: "Choose this day whom you will serve. . . . But as for me and my house, we will serve the LORD" (Josh. 24:15). Now again the people stood at a crossroad between the paths of obedience or unfaithfulness, blessing or curse.

The fateful scene begins in 1 Samuel 8, when a demand was pressed upon the prophet, a demand that broke Samuel's heart and spoke of bitter things yet to come. At issue was Samuel's old age and the lack of qualified leaders to follow him. Therefore the elders of the people came to him, saying, "Behold, you are old and your sons do not walk in your ways. Now appoint for us a king to judge us like all the nations" (1 Sam. 8:5).

In those seemingly innocuous words lay a dreadful affront not just to Samuel but to the Lord. As we saw in Deuteronomy, Israel already had a king, one not appointed by man but one who held his throne by divine authority and saving grace. The Lord was king over Israel; yet these elders—appointed to serve on the Lord's behalf—disloyally sought a human king, the kind of king "all the nations" had.

We can understand how shocked Samuel must have been. What a bitter chapter so late in his faithful and effective ministry! His lament is recorded in 1 Samuel 8:6-7:

But the thing displeased Samuel when they said, "Give us a king to judge us." And Samuel prayed to the LORD. And the LORD said to Samuel, "Obey the voice of the people in all that they say to you, for they have not rejected you, but they have rejected me from being king over them."

Both Samuel and the Lord understood this request as a denial of the two chief principles of Deuteronomy. First, the Israelites turned their hearts from the devotion God demanded, formally demanding a king in place of the Lord. Second, they repudiated the mandate to holiness, to separation from the other nations in all of their ways. They had married with the people around them, they had taken their idols as gods, and now they demanded a king "such as all the other nations have" (NIV).

Faithfulness to God and separation from the world are inseparably linked. The vertical dimension of devotion to the Lord and the horizontal axis of holiness before the world either stand or fall together. Indeed, a synergy exists between the two, both in standing and in falling. What is it that emboldens God's people to stand before a world of sin and unbelief, faithfully shunning its ways and holding fast to the ways of God? Only a fervent relationship with God and a keen devotion to Him alone empowers the call to holiness. Yet it is also true that a shunning of the ways of the world, a separation from its treasures and pleasures, its religions and philosophies, equally sustains us in our fidelity to God. Faithfulness to God and holiness before the world are inseparable and mutually supportive, but in reverse they each lend momentum to the failure of the other. This describes what happened in Israel. They forgot the Lord and therefore sought out the world. Fellowship with the world led to the worship of its gods, which drew their hearts further from the true and saving God and further into pagan ways. In this manner God's holy people became an unbelieving nation. All this culminated in the demand for a king, a human leader "such as all the other nations have," in the place of God.

Faithfulness to God and separation from the world are inseparably linked. The vertical dimension of devotion to the Lord and the horizontal axis of holiness before the world either stand or fall together.

This principle holds true today. Churches that lose their focus on God inevitably become worldly in their practice, which leads them further from God until there is hardly anything distinctly Christian left. But those who make the knowledge and glory of God their prime focus are pulled back from the world with its methods and its gods and are thus drawn closer in reliance on and fellowship with the Lord.

A GENERATION THAT DID NOT KNOW GOD

What started this process in motion? At the critical juncture with which the book of Judges begins, we gain our answer and a lesson for the church today: "There arose another generation after them who did not know the LORD or the work that he had done for Israel. And the people of Israel did what was evil in the sight of the LORD and served the Baals" (Judg. 2:10-11). Among all the issues, this is the key, according to the biblical record: People or churches who forget the Lord and all that He has done inevitably fall away into the ways and worship of the world. Deuteronomy solemnly warned: "And when the LORD your God brings you into the land that he swore to your fathers, to Abraham, to Isaac, and to Jacob, to give you—with great and good cities that you did not build, and houses full of all good things that you did not fill, and cisterns that you did not dig, and vineyards and olive trees that you did not plant—and when you eat and are full, *then take care lest you forget the LORD*, who brought you out of the land of Egypt, out of the house of slavery" (Deut. 6:10-12). The key to faithfulness is knowing God, and the key to knowing God, according to Deuteronomy, is knowing salvation history as taught in the Bible, and through that history knowing God Himself. Deuteronomy 6:20-23, given to the people at so critical a time, made this the vital concern for years to come:

> *"When your son asks you in time to come, 'What is the meaning of the testimonies and the statutes and the rules that the LORD our God has commanded you?' then you shall say to your son, 'We were Pharaoh's slaves in Egypt. And the LORD brought us out of Egypt with a mighty hand. And the LORD showed signs and wonders, great and grievous, against Egypt and against Pharaoh and all his household, before our eyes. And he brought us out from there, that he might bring us in and give us the land that he swore to give to our fathers."*

Why, then, did the people forget the Lord? The Bible does not give us all the details, but the picture is clear enough. They became caught up with the business of the world. They had entered into the land of promise, a land "with great and good cities that you did not build, and houses full of all good things that you did not fill, and cisterns that you did not dig, and vineyards and olive trees that you did not plant" (Deut. 6:10-11), and they set about the various pursuits appropriate to their setting. Some of them took up trades, as well they should, and others set about organizing the new cities and towns and tribal holdings. All of this would have been hard work, and when they gathered together on the Lord's day, they had much on their minds. I think we can imagine the Levite of that day, stepping up to the ancient equivalent of the pulpit to speak to the people. Before and after his message he would have heard the kind of advice preachers get today, heeding it only at great danger to their flock: "Pastor, give us something relevant. We don't need theology and doctrine, but instead practical things to help us do better in our lives."

This is the key: People or churches who do not know the Lord and all that He has done inevitably fall away into the ways and worship of the world.

It is always a temptation to believe that knowledge of God is impractical, of little value in our lives. Our sinful nature conspires with worldly influences to lead our attention away from God and to ourselves—our work, our relationships, our hobbies, our difficulties. These are the important things, says the folly in our hearts. But the story of Israel tells us that nothing is more practical to the people of God, nothing more essential, nothing more fruitful or beneficial than the knowledge of God and His ways in salvation. This is what Israel needed to hear preached, just as we need it today. This is what they needed to study, this was the true and great pursuit of their age, as it is in every age: to know the Lord, to remember the living God, to hold fast to His saving works, and to pass this faith on to their children as the most vital legacy one could possibly leave. This is why Jesus said, in His great High-Priestly prayer to the Father, "And this is eternal life, that they may know you the only true God, and Jesus Christ whom you have sent" (John 17:3). It is evident that the nation forgot this. In the prophecy of Deuteronomy

28:47 God bluntly explains the failure and subsequent woe that came upon Israel: "because you did not serve the LORD your God with joyfulness and gladness of heart, because of the abundance of all things."

The story of Israel tells us that there is nothing more practical to the people of God, nothing more essential, nothing more fruitful or beneficial than the knowledge of God and His ways in salvation.

The lesson for us is plain. Deformation starts with the failure to proclaim the knowledge of God and His salvation. The pressing need of any day is preaching and teaching that is about God and not about man, that focuses on salvation from sin and not on solutions to the issues and problems reported in the newspapers and magazines. We often hear complaints about one whose thoughts are fixed on God: "He is too heavenly-minded to be any earthly good." Yet the record of Israel in her fall says that it is only the heavenly-minded who remember the Lord, from whom all blessings flow to them that love Him. I recently heard an older minister comment that he wasn't sure from his experience if it was true that the heavenly-minded are of less earthly value, but he had learned unfailingly that those who are earthly-minded are never of any heavenly good at all.

The clear lesson from the story of Israel is this: The first work of the church is always to teach about God and His great saving deeds. This must take precedence over every competing value, including the church's mandate to service and good deeds.

The pressing need of any day is preaching and teaching that is about God and not about man, that focuses on salvation from sin and not on problems reported in the newspapers and magazines.

The New Testament records Jesus' adherence to this priority. Mark records that early in our Lord's ministry, crowds of needy people thronged to receive His healing and blessing. Jesus withdrew from them, spending a morning in prayer. It was Simon Peter who found Him, astonished that Jesus would miss so great an opportunity to grow His ministry. "Everyone is looking for you," Peter exclaimed. Jesus' reply is telling and one that sets an agenda consistent with our Old Testament study. "He said to them, 'Let us go on to the next towns, that I may preach there also, for that is why I came out'" (Mark 1:35-39). Jesus' own ministry, for all the fantastic miracles He performed, first and foremost sought to teach about God and His kingdom, so that people might know the Lord and be saved.

THE PEOPLE'S CHOICE

"We want a king over us. Then we will be like all the other nations!" That was the people's cry, and God in His judgment gave them what they wanted. Samuel warned them that if they wanted a worldly king and a worldly religion, along with it they would gain the worldly way of life with all its bitterness and woe. Samuel warned them that no earthly king either would or could care for them the way the Lord did; rather he would use them and exploit them in his own pursuit of worldly security and success. Still the people cried out for a king. Finally the Lord said to Samuel, "Obey their voice and make them a king" (1 Sam. 8:22).

So Samuel went to find and anoint the king who fit this bill. His name was Saul, and his description in the Bible fits the worldly aspirations of the people. He was "a handsome young man. There was not a man among the people of Israel more handsome than he. From his shoulders upward he was taller than any of the people" (1 Sam. 9:2). Notice how external all this is; Saul's qualifications were all on the outside. What he lacked in compassion and conviction, in faith and devotion, he made up in physical stature and good looks. Let us understand that this is what God gives to those who seek the kings of this world, the riches of this world, worldly success and worldly praise. Saul would lead the people, and he would do so with great ability. His reign would last forty years and would include many notable triumphs. Yet they would all be worldly triumphs, external gains, while the heart and soul of the people withered and shrank and true divine blessings became a dimmer and dimmer memory from an age gone by. What Saul offered the people can be had by the church as well—visible and glittering success as measured and admired by the world, but always with the same cost.

Whenever a generation of God's people forgets the Lord and instead looks to the world for its solutions and models, there are Sauls waiting to be brought forward. As in Israel's case, we should suspect God's judgment whenever a leader like Saul comes to the fore—one with great gifts and attractive ability who practices a worldly gospel of success and fleshly glory. The example of Saul, admired by men but rejected by God (1 Sam. 13:14), exhorts us to measure our success in the church not in terms of numbers or money or political strength—the kinds of things the Sauls of the world provide—but in the knowledge of God, in our devotion to Him, and in our holiness before the world. It is the faithful and blessed church that can say with Moses: "They followed in your steps, receiving direction from you. . . . Thus the LORD became king in Jeshurun, when the heads of the people were gathered, all the tribes of Israel together" (Deut. 33:3-5).

3

THE WISDOM OF SOLOMON

Israel's tale of deformation has many beginnings. It is also a story with many fathers, and in the passing of the throne from one father to his son we find another great moment in deformation history.

The fate of the Old Testament nation was largely determined by the spiritual condition of individual men, especially its kings. This is why one of the main records of this time is called "The Book of the Kings." In 1 and 2 Kings we find ourselves reading with bated breath as one king dies and another enters the scene. In the Deuteronomic History, which runs from the entry into the land to the exile from it, the difference between reading "the king did what was right in the eyes of the LORD" and "he did evil in the eyes of the LORD" is great and significant indeed.

LIKE FATHER, LIKE SON

We left off our story with the reign of King Saul, the king "like all the nations." Though Saul reigned for forty years, God was gracious in replacing him with "a man after his own heart" (1 Sam. 13:14). The selection of King David tells us what we need to know about God's intention. The Lord sent Samuel to the house of Jesse, where each of the man's sons were paraded before the prophet. "Surely the LORD's anointed is before all," thought the prophet as the eldest and most impressive came by. But God reproved him, with words that are as famous as they are sadly neglected today: "Do not look on his appearance or on the height of his stature, because I have rejected him. For the LORD sees not as man sees: man looks on the outward appearance, but the LORD looks on the heart" (1 Sam. 16:6-7).

David's father had not even thought it necessary to bring his

younger child before the man of God, but Samuel insisted, and God
revealed that David was His choice. With a beginning like this, it is no
wonder that David's career is synonymous with godly, servant leadership. His greatest moments were marked by humble submission coupled
with bold faith in the grace and power of God. Both against the giant
Philistine warrior Goliath and against the jealous, evil King Saul, David
set an inspiring example of courage and faith until God finally put him
in place on Israel's throne.

One lesson that comes through in the Old Testament is that God's
people do not often handle success very well. Sadly, David was no exception, and at the height of his glory he fell swiftly and stunningly into
adultery, betrayal, and murder. David was brought to repentance, but
his reign never regained its earlier glory. The effects of his sin were particularly revealed in the character of his sons who, like many children of
great fathers they hardly know, picked up David's flaws while neglect-
ing his many great virtues. One was a rapist and another a murderer. All
of them, it seems, were schemers. Absalom, who was especially precious
to David's heart, raised a rebellion against his father and died in battle
against David's army. While elderly David tottered on the brink of death,
another son, Adonijah, conspired with many of David's close officials
to displace the king and his appointed successor, Solomon.

The final chapters of David's chronicle, found in 1 and 2 Samuel,
give a decidedly mixed review of his reign. On the one hand we have
great songs of praise and faith in God, in 2 Samuel 22—23. Chapter 24,
the last chapter in 2 Samuel, counters with a narrative of David's cen-
sus, which God punished as an act of faithless trust in human power. The
David pictured is one whose heart is with the Lord, but who has lost the
clarity and faith of his earlier triumphs. Whereas young David had
proved a paragon of heroic faith and passion, elder David resorted to
mere pragmatism in the place of godly principle.

I said that the passing of the throne from father to son provides a
vital moment in Old Testament history, and in that respect David's
charge to his son and successor, Solomon, presents one of the most dis-
heartening scenes from his life. How wonderful it would be for David
to go out with a blazing devotion to the Lord, with a stake planted in
the ground that others could later rally around. Sadly, in 1 Kings 2 we
read words that reflect the competing spirits of David's latter reign. "Be
strong, and show yourself a man," said the great king, beginning

strongly, "and keep the charge of the LORD your God, walking in his ways and keeping his statutes, his commandments . . . that you may prosper in all that you do and wherever you turn" (1 Kings 2:2-3). Then, as if he had not even heard the words he just had spoken, David directed Solomon to murder all his rivals and begin his reign with a sword bathed in blood. How distressing to hear David call for vengeance on those who had wronged him. One man had committed the sin of cursing at David earlier in life, and the aged king commanded his petty revenge: "Bring his gray head down with blood to Sheol" (v. 9).

David shows us what one man of faith may accomplish. How often he soared by faith where few of us dare to go, especially in his younger years. But David also shows us that no man—not one of us—is immune from the demons of our sinful nature. Exposed by his position and surely by his pride, David's fall into sin was steep and devastating, with effects he never really shook. It is striking that a man like David not only left a legacy of principle, but also of unbelieving pragmatism; not merely of faith and reliance on God, but also of fleshly self-reliance and worldly use of power. If this could happen to David, how much more likely is it of the lesser souls who lead our churches today, unless they stand upon God's Word. In the final analysis, David reminds us that no matter how godly or great a man may be, there is only One on whom he may utterly rely. We must always put our ultimate trust not in David but in David's son, not the one born in a palace but in a humble manger, not from Bathsheba but from the virgin womb of Mary. Whereas David's victories led to failure, Jesus' defeat on the cross led Him to victory, His death to life, His humility to heavenly exaltation. No merely human leader can ever take the place of a saving God, and David reminds us to trust in Him alone.

Whereas David's victories led to failure, Jesus' defeat on the cross led Him to victory, His death to life, His humility to heavenly exaltation. No merely human leader can ever take the place of a saving God.

HOW WISE WAS SOLOMON?

Many, no doubt, looked with great hope upon David's son, Solomon, who succeeded him to the throne in Jerusalem. Solomon's very name speaks of peace and wisdom from God. In the blessings that came to

Israel through his reign, he in many ways foretells the splendor of the reign of Christ. In anticipation of our Lord, Solomon built the temple in Jerusalem. His throne and his glory are types of Christ and His kingdom. Solomon made a great speech at the dedication of that temple that is a model of prayer and worship. Truly there is hardly a greater name in all the Old Testament than that of Solomon, whose reign alone rivals the days of Joshua, when God's favor boldly shone upon the Promised Land.

With all that, however, Solomon's reign also marked a new beginning in the history of Israel's deformation. There is little doubt—and it is clear that this is the view of the writer of 1 and 2 Kings—that Israel's freefall into deformation and judgment begins anew with wise King Solomon.

We see this downfall in the sad commentary that begins in chapter 11 of 1 Kings, telling of Solomon's many wives and reminding us of David's greatest sin:

> *Now King Solomon loved many foreign women, along with the daughter of Pharaoh: Moabite, Ammonite, Edomite, Sidonian, and Hittite women, from the nations concerning which the LORD had said to the people of Israel, "You shall not enter into marriage with them, neither shall they with you, for surely they will turn away your heart after their gods." Solomon clung to these in love. He had 700 wives, princesses, and 300 concubines. And his wives turned away his heart.*
>
> —1 KINGS 11:1-3

This passage refers to God's command regarding marriage with the pagan nations, a prohibition Solomon must not have applied to himself. Yet, if he had consulted God's charter for Israel, the book of Deuteronomy, he would have discovered quite a few restraints that would have saved him a great deal of trouble. Solomon likely knew of these clear commands, but in his pride he disobeyed the Lord. Here is what Deuteronomy commanded as safeguards against an excess of royal pride and power: "He must not acquire many horses for himself or cause the people to return to Egypt in order to acquire many horses, since the LORD has said to you, 'You shall never return that way again.' And he shall not acquire many wives for himself, lest his heart turn away, nor shall he acquire for himself excessive silver and gold" (Deut. 17:16-17).

All these were hallmarks of Solomon's reign, and thus we sense trouble coming, which is exactly what the continuing account of 1 Kings relates:

> *For when Solomon was old his wives turned away his heart after other gods, and his heart was not wholly true to the LORD his God, as was the heart of David his father. For Solomon went after Ashtoreth the goddess of the Sidonians, and after Milcom the abomination of the Ammonites. So Solomon did what was evil in the sight of the LORD and did not wholly follow the Lord, as David his father had done. Then Solomon built a high place for Chemosh the abomination of Moab, and for Molech the abomination of the Ammonites, on the mountain east of Jerusalem. And so he did for all his foreign wives, who made offerings and sacrificed to their gods.*
>
> —1 KINGS 11:4-8

This is *wise* King Solomon! I have often wondered how one gifted with supernatural wisdom could plunge so deeply into folly. Clearly, wisdom is not enough. Wisdom does not replace faith and obedience to God's Word. No man, not even wise King Solomon, can safely advance beyond the teaching of God's Word. Solomon ignored God's commands, and in the folly that resulted from his sin these words formed the epitaph on his otherwise glorious reign:

> *And the LORD was angry with Solomon, because his heart had turned away from the LORD, the God of Israel, who had appeared to him twice and had commanded him concerning this thing, that he should not go after other gods. But he did not keep what the LORD commanded. Therefore the LORD said to Solomon, "Since this has been your practice and you have not kept my covenant and my statutes that I have commanded you, I will surely tear the kingdom from you and will give it to your servant. Yet for the sake of David your father I will not do it in your days, but I will tear it out of the hand of your son."*
>
> —1 KINGS 11:9-12

We can learn innumerable lessons from wise King Solomon. He shows us again that disobedience on the horizontal level—that is, an unwillingness to be different from the world and its ways, to be biblically restrained and shaped in our lifestyle—always leads to unfaithfulness on the vertical level. He took foreign wives, the loveliest daughters of Egypt and Moab, Ammon and Sidonia, and in so doing took their gods into his heart. Surely Solomon thought that he would win them to the Lord, just as countless other amorous fools have believed after him, assuming that his wisdom and godliness exempted him from what God had commanded to lesser souls (and kings).

What is true for others was true for Solomon: Unbelief and disobedience are not the pathways to blessing but to judgment from God. Solomon thought it safe—wise and spiritual as he was—to give himself to riches and worldly power, to palaces and fleets of horses and the fleshly embrace of 700 lovers. But God's Word stood firm in his case as in every other, and the wages of sin were written in spiritual death. It was not long, having trusted his own wisdom in place of the Lord's, having served his sinful desires instead of the will of God, before Solomon was rationalizing the construction of shrines to Baal and statues of Molech, no doubt in the spirit of religious tolerance and generosity. What a warning this example is to every spiritual leader, to think that it was Solomon, in all his wisdom and prestige and glory, who erected the idols on the hills and in the temple at Jerusalem.

Disobedience on the horizontal level always leads to unfaithfulness on the vertical level. Solomon thought himself above God's Word, and it was not long before he was rationalizing the construction of shrines to Baal and statues of Molech.

THE PRAGMATIC YARDSTICK

Of all the lessons Solomon provides, none is more relevant to our own time than one of the great levers of deformation—namely, the use of the pragmatic yardstick. To get at this, let me make one simple observation: Solomon engaged in the most heinous forms of idolatry. "Solomon went after Ashtoreth the goddess of the Sidonians, and after Milcom the abomination of the Ammonites. . . . Then Solomon built a high place for Chemosh the abomination of Moab, and for Molech the abomination of the Ammonites, on the mountain east of Jerusalem" (1 Kings 11:5-7). Yet nowhere do we read that God removed His blessing from Solomon and his kingdom. Quite the contrary! The great summary of

Solomon's reign comes just before this record of his idolatry, but chronologically they overlap:

> *King Solomon excelled all the kings of the earth in riches and in wisdom. And the whole earth sought the presence of Solomon to hear his wisdom, which God had put into his mind. Every one of them brought his present, articles of silver and gold, garments, myrrh, spices, horses, and mules, so much year by year.*
> —1 KINGS 10:23-25

All this time Solomon was being blessed abundantly beyond all imagination. Yet if we take this to be a divine endorsement of his actions and attitudes, we are sadly mistaken. Nonetheless, this is the kind of argument used to justify any number of unbiblical methods of church growth and success today. We hear this justification for the grossest abuses, the most blatant disregard for biblical teaching: "God seems to be blessing it." Use of the pragmatic yardstick instead of the biblical yardstick—what we think is right in terms of means and ends rather than what God has said is right—is one of the great and enduring principles of deformation.

We hear this justification for any number of unbiblical methods and approaches to church growth and success: "It is working"; "God is blessing it"; "Things are going well."

"It is working"; "God is blessing it"; "Things are going well." Certainly we should not automatically be against things working or against God's blessing, against things succeeding in tangible ways. Yet success—particularly as measured in temporal or worldly terms such as size, wealth, or prestige—should not determine how we are to serve and worship God, but rather faithfulness to Him through obedience to His Word.

Is there much doubt what was said to any who complained against Solomon's idolatry? One might have come forward to object, "Look, this is a terrible abomination and an offense before the Lord! You are doing the very things God has forbidden!" And what would he have been told? "What are you talking about? All is well! How can you complain when Solomon is becoming greater and richer and smarter and more glorious day by day? It is working, so it must be right!" This is the pragmatic yardstick, which holds a treasured place in vast numbers of churches today, just as in Solomon's kingdom before.

Why, we ask, did God bless Solomon even when Solomon followed after foreign women and worshiped foreign gods? The Bible gives the reason clearly: "For the sake of David your father" (1 Kings 11:12). God's condemnation of Solomon's sin is plainly given; yet the Lord forestalled His wrath because of His own grace and faithfulness. "I will surely tear the kingdom from you," God threatened Solomon, but with this qualification: "Yet for the sake of David your father I will not do it in your days, but I will tear it out of the hand of your son" (vv. 11-12).

God is rich in mercy, abounding in grace, slow to anger, and quick to bless those who are His own. But that does not justify our rejection of His ways as prescribed in the Bible. And yet wherever deformation takes place, this pragmatic argument will consistently be used to defend it.

This is the logic employed today by those who advocate vast worldly agendas as the means of providing church growth and success. The logic of this movement is intensely pragmatic, and admittedly so. Its advocates hail their success in "reaching multitudes" for Christ, and their methods are justified on the basis of pragmatic achievements— numbers, money, influence, and prestige—rather than on biblical warrant. I have heard it said, accurately enough, that church success today is measured in terms of simple ABC's: attendance, buildings, and cash. In support of these goals, churches turn to marketing in place of ministry, entertainment in place of worship, the shearing of worldly goats instead of the feeding of God's sheep.

Church growth consultants and leaders often have excellent practical advice that is worth hearing; certainly there are practical ways in which the church can and should learn from worldly sources. There is nothing wrong, for instance, with running an efficient parking lot. But having defined success in terms of worldly ABC's, an increasing number of evangelical churches today have necessarily succumbed to the pragmatic worldly means needed to achieve them, especially by marketing goods and services and by presenting attractive entertainment in the church.

This is not to say that modern pragmatists do not look to the Bible or cite biblical precedents, for they do. On the whole, however, their literature combines creative exegesis with a blatantly pragmatic logic. For instance, we find a classic support for their emphasis on attracting masses of people in the miracle where Jesus fed 5,000 people at one time, that number counting only the men. Wasn't Jesus winsome and attractive, drawing to Himself multitudes? Shouldn't we, too, craft our methods to bring multitudes into our churches?

This argument, however, fails to add that Jesus' subsequent preaching—a message that emphasized God's sovereign grace and Jesus' own atoning death—drove away those crowds until only twelve people remained. Far from pandering to or entertaining those who gathered before him, Jesus preached a Gospel that was and is offensive to the masses. "Truly, truly, I say to you," He told them, "unless you eat the flesh of the Son of Man and drink his blood, you have no life in you. Whoever feeds on my flesh and drinks my blood has eternal life, and I will raise him up on the last day. For my flesh is true food, and my blood is true drink" (John 6:53-55). How is that for "relevant, accepting, seeker-sensitive preaching"?

Jesus' preaching drove away the crowds until basically only twelve remained. Jesus preached a Gospel that was and is offensive to the masses.

Surely we must preach Christ's free offer of salvation with an aim to reach many with and for the Gospel. The offense of the Gospel must never be us and our ingrown indifference to the lost, but rather Christ and His cross. Surely we must tell the greatest story ever told with joy and confidence in God's love for hundreds and thousands and millions. But with that sincerely said, let us notice that Jesus' preaching did the very opposite thing church growth experts advocate, as seen in the multitudes' response to His preaching of the Gospel. Even His closest followers were disturbed, as their reply makes clear: "This is a hard saying; who can listen to it?" the disciples complained. "Do you want to go away as well?" Jesus replied. Peter's answer is immortal and more precious than the mere applause of many thousands: "Lord, to whom shall we go? You have the words of eternal life" (John 6:60, 67-68).

Today's church marketers look for consumers to convert into customers. But Jesus looked upon sinners and sought to be their Savior. He sought not customers but disciples; He came not to sell but to purchase with His blood.

What is the lesson? Whereas today's church marketers look upon the world as consumers, whom they would convert into much-admired customers of their goods and services, Jesus looked upon sinners and sought to be their Savior. Jesus sought not customers but disciples; He sought not to sell something to the masses but to purchase with His blood those God had given Him and was calling through the Gospel. We do His work best today when we are willing to lose a few thousand customers for the sake of the few disciples God has brought to faith through His Word.

Church growth advocates would reply that far too many churches devote themselves to the Bible but are indifferent to the masses of people outside their doors. If that is true, the medicine the pragmatists prescribe can only kill the patient. A healthy church is one devoted to God and thus to His Word, even as Moses insisted on the Plains of Moab, and not to the tastes and felt needs of unbelieving neighbors. A godly church is one that, far from mimicking the styles and methods of the pagan world, stands apart in its reverence and holiness, both of which must profoundly shape both form and substance. As I put it earlier, the godly church is driven by a centripetal, not a centrifugal, force; its identity, mission, and methods are derived from Christ, so that His followers shine a light that is truly His into the darkness of the world.

Neither of these priorities—devotion to God and holiness in the world—stand opposed to true evangelistic zeal, but rather are the source and venue for God's display of saving grace through our worship and witness. If we are to save many *to* Christ and His Gospel—and let that be our prayer—let us save them *with* Christ and His Gospel. For to save many *with* anything other than the proclamation of Christ crucified—be it gripping music, engaging drama, or meaningful community—is to save them *to* something very different than the salvation Jesus offers sinners with His blood. For what we save them *with*, we always save them *to*.

If we are to save many to Christ and His Gospel, let us save them with Christ and His Gospel. For what we save them with, we always save them to.

So flippant are many church growth appeals to biblical support that I have actually read in one best-selling tome an appeal to Mark 12:37 to justify an emphasis on numbers and excitement. That verse tells of the masses that attended Jesus' preaching at the temple in Jerusalem shortly after his triumphal entry: "The large crowd listened to [Jesus] with delight" (NIV). What is forgotten, however, is that in a couple of short days that very crowd would shout out to Pontius Pilate, "Crucify Him! Crucify Him!" (Mark 15:8ff.).[1] Despite what I am convinced are laudable motives and an earnest desire to counteract a very real deadness in so many churches today, the church growth pragmatists threaten to do to the church what this crowd once did to Jesus.

Like Solomon, the real problem is our self-reliant pride—a pride that says that what God commands doesn't really apply to us. If we glimpsed just a portion of the sin and idolatry and folly that resides within our deceitful hearts—and so often it is this very reality we forget—then we would tremble to truly innovate beyond the methods and means of God's Word, lest we, like Solomon, erect pagan idols within the house of the holy God.

Many church growth books contain a useful critique of our lack of evangelistic fervor and provide thoughtful practical advice on how to remove needless barriers to the unchurched around us. But let us simply observe that we find also consistent examples of the pragmatic yardstick in the church growth movement. Pragmatism happens when we do things because they seem good to us, because they seem to work, whether or not they are commanded in God's Word. Whenever our practices justify themselves or we use shoddy exegesis to justify them, we risk a path of ruinous logic that leads away from real obedience to God and the true spiritual blessing that comes only from Him. Instead of resenting biblical critique, as the pragmatists tend to do, we should each be open to and even embrace constructive criticism that comes from the Word of God.

I am persuaded that the majority of those who have adopted church growth pragmatism have done so with laudable motives. They want to reach multitudes who are lost and to see the church restored to prominence in our communities. But following in the wake of several generations of mass revivalism—of which they are the modern-day representatives—they have built a strategy based on its greatest flaws. Among these are an overly optimistic and unbiblical view of man in sin, for whom they think salvation is an almost mechanical process and one that can succeed through gimmicks and sentimental appeals without the regenerating work of the Holy Spirit as He bears witness to the Word. Coupled with this is a small view of God, and one that especially minimizes the implications of His holy character. In such a scheme the cross—both Christ's and ours—is a scandal not to sinners but to the church, which replaces it with a false gospel of success and temporal happiness. Seeking to save people *with* a gospel of fleeting experiences or therapeutic self-help or glitzy sentimentality, such churches simply are bound to fail to save them *to* the thrice holy God of the Bible and the salvation that is of heaven and not of the earth.

Pragmatism occurs in every age of the church, always pleading for worldly rather than biblical means and ends. Does this mean, therefore, that faithful churches have no room for new ideas or that we should never adapt to a changing cultural landscape? Not at all. Christians and churches will always make any number of decisions relating to practical issues. Biblical Christianity must never be pragmatic, yet always is practical. One of the exciting aspects of life in the church is the constant need for new ideas, new approaches, new solutions to problems unique to our setting and place. Yet for all of our practical and prayerful ingenuity, Christians must also proceed with principled rather than pragmatic decisions, with faithfulness to God's Word rather than fascination with apparent signs of success. We must hold fast to the very principles God gave through Moses on the fields of Moab—to exclusive devotion to God and not to the gods of this world, to holiness before the world so that we are willing and even determined to be different, to a salvation that is by grace alone through the blood of our sacrifice, Jesus Christ, received through faith alone in the message of His Gospel.

In this path of faithfulness, not success, we today may be wiser even than Solomon. True biblical wisdom begins by realizing that on our own we are not wise, that we need to be instructed by God in spiritual things. As the psalmist said in words echoed later by Solomon himself: "The fear of the LORD is the beginning of wisdom; all those who practice it have a good understanding" (Ps. 111:10).

> *On our own we are not wise; we need to be instructed by God in spiritual things. What we think bodes well for the future often bodes ill. We are children, unable on our own to think rightly in spiritual affairs; we are sinners, unqualified to judge right from wrong on our own.*

Surely no better safeguard against idolatry and folly exists than a healthy awareness of our propensity to sin. We simply are not qualified to make judgments about spiritual matters without the guardrails of God's sure revelation. What we in our wisdom think bodes well for the future often bodes ill. We are children, unable on our own to think rightly in spiritual affairs; we are sinners, unqualified to judge right from wrong without help from the holy God through His Spirit and His Word. Let us heed, then, the words of Isaiah, who also realized his sin and thus depended on God and His Word:

> *Seek the* LORD *while he may be found; call upon him while he is near. . . . For my thoughts are not your thoughts, neither are your ways my ways, declares the* LORD. *For as the heavens are higher than the earth, so are my ways higher than your ways and my thoughts than your thoughts.*
>
> —ISA. 55:6-9.

Solomon had a near-perfect mental instrument; yet like our smaller minds it was governed by a wicked, deceitful heart. Let us not think, therefore, that we are up to the task of judging between good and evil, between right and wrong, apart from our total dependence on the Bible. Whenever we, like Solomon, lay our hand upon the pragmatic yardstick instead of on the perfect Word of God, we open the door to the folly and sin that ever mark the way of our wicked human race.

Let us therefore not envy Solomon his apparent success, for its cost was high in future woe. Solomon did not pay for his sins; his generation did not taste the bitter waters for his deformation from the principles of God's Word. But the next generation paid mightily under his son, who was neither so wise nor so blessed by the favor of God. So might it be for the offspring of our pragmatic generation, who will drink bitter waters for what our generation of the church is doing in its perversion of worship and teaching, in our marketing of religion instead of proclaiming a gospel of life to sinners who are dying, in our craving for success at the expense of our duty of faithfulness to God. What might have been had Solomon sent his wives away, torn down his gaudy palace, and destroyed the idols of the foreign gods we can only guess, though surely it would have pleased the Lord. If we will be willing to repent of our sin in similar ways, it is surely not too late for God to restore to our churches what only He can give, the heavenly blessings of true spiritual life.

4

THE NEW AGAINST THE OLD

One of the more enigmatic passages in the Old Testament concerns the man of God from Judah who appears and disappears in 1 Kings 13. This figure plays a transitional role in the story of Israel's deformation, making a vital point about the binding character of God's revelation. Through this man and two other transitional figures, Rehoboam king of Judah and Jeroboam king of Israel, the Bible makes a vital statement about the new against the old in matters of faith.

THE FOLLY OF YOUTH

God had told Solomon that for the sake of his father his throne would not be taken during his lifetime. However, God immediately began to set the stage for what was to come by stirring up opposition to Solomon, including a rebellion led by Jeroboam, son of Nebat. Jeroboam was an able man from a prominent family in the tribe of Joseph, and God promised him that after Solomon's death he would receive the kingdom God would take from Solomon's son. Learning of this, Solomon sought out Jeroboam's life, but the would-be usurper escaped to Egypt to await his time.

Solomon died after reigning forty years, like his father David and like Saul before him. The succession fell to his son Rehoboam, and a delegation from the people immediately confronted their new king. Rehoboam was in a difficult position. During the last years of his reign Solomon had been excessively harsh in his work demands. Furthermore, a rift between the northern and the southern tribes, one that went back at least as far as the conflict between Saul and David, threatened to flare up again. It is interesting that the people gathered at Shechem, one of the main meeting places in the north, to entreat Rehoboam. In this way, they were sending a message of warning to the vulnerable southerner who came to be crowned as king. The delegation was led by Jeroboam, who had returned to capitalize on the situation. They complained, "Your father made our yoke heavy. Now therefore lighten the hard service of your father and his heavy yoke on us, and we will serve you" (1 Kings 12:4).

The verses that follow give us access into Rehoboam's decision-making process, one that pits the young against the aged, the new against the old. Seeking advice, he took three days to consult two groups of people, one comprised of the elders who had served his father Solomon, the other a group of young men who had grown up with him. The old men counseled a course of godly humility, servant leadership, and moderation in his exercise of power. "If you will be a servant to this people today and serve them, and speak good words to them when you answer them, then they will be your servants forever," the elders advised (v. 7). Rehoboam, however, rejected this counsel, and we get the impression that he did so rudely. Instead, he turned to his youthful friends, who offered different advice altogether, urging the king to approach the delegation with an arrogant and imperial tone. "Thus shall you speak to this people who said to you, 'Your father made our yoke heavy, but you lighten it for us,' thus shall you say to them, 'My little finger is thicker than my father's thighs. And now, whereas my father laid on you a heavy yoke, I will add to your yoke. My father disciplined you with whips, but I will discipline you with scorpions'" (vv. 10-11).

After three days the delegation led by Jeroboam returned, as requested. Rehoboam foolishly followed the advice of his young friends and haughtily asserted his authority over the people. The result was disastrous. First Kings 12:16 tells us, "And when all Israel saw that the king did not listen to them, the people answered the king, 'What portion do we have in David? We have no inheritance in the son of Jesse. To your tents, O Israel! Look now to your own house, David!'" Rehoboam had not reckoned with the fact that without the consent of the people he could not rule, and his subsequent attempts to force himself on them met with failure. Jeroboam was swiftly crowned king over the ten northern tribes of Israel, and Rehoboam retreated to Jerusalem with only a fraction of his father's realm intact.

This episode completes what had gone before; what happened to Rehoboam had as much to do with his father as with him. In the long view of the biblical record we see how one generation's compromise impacts another. Church history reveals the same, and we need to reflect on how our actions will impact the generation of our children. How short a time it was between the high days of Solomon's glory and might and Rehoboam's loss of the kingdom! "This is My doing," God said to him in essence, and as Jesus' letters to the seven churches show, God still judges His people according to their faithfulness or disobedience. If there are to be lampstands burning in our churches in years to come, it will be because we took a principled stand of faith today.

Furthermore, we see in Rehoboam how far the house of David had declined in a mere three generations. Rehoboam's failure had its roots in David's great sin with Bathsheba and the turmoil into which that cast his family. Solomon, for his part, was busy enjoying his riches and concubines rather than seeing to the future of the kingdom. It is no wonder, given the example of his father, that when the young King Rehoboam was advised to act as a servant leader, he abhorred the very idea.

But the main point of this account is to present a contrast between the old and the new. The old is here associated with wisdom, with humble strength, with godly moderation. Not surprisingly, the elders' advice hearkens back to God's instructions in Deuteronomy. There the king was told to study the Scriptures in order to gain the very attitude these elders were advising. He was "to fear the LORD his God by keeping all the words of this law and these statutes, and doing them, that his heart may not be lifted up above his brothers . . . so that he may continue long in his kingdom, he and his children, in Israel" (Deut. 17:19-20). The course of the old and wise would lead to longevity and prosperity. Rehoboam, however, chose the young and new, and these are here aligned with a lack of devotion to God, with folly and arrogant pride, and ultimately with ruin in the loss of the throne he had received. Deformation found its place in the life of the nation only after it first was lodged in the heart of the king.

The real problem was that Rehoboam himself was estranged from God. During those three tense days of deliberation we do not once see Rehoboam praying to the Lord or seeking wisdom from the Scriptures. He saw only the political dynamics of his situation, forgetting the spiritual relationship with God that was available to him. Rehoboam did not pray, did not seek wisdom in God's Word, and did not even heed the advice of the elders; and in this way he brought himself and his cause to ruin. In the New Testament James exhorts believers to seek wisdom from God: "If any of you lacks wisdom, let him ask God, who gives generously to all without reproach, and it will be given him" (Jas. 1:5). In contrast, Rehoboam exemplifies the warning given in Isaiah 30:1: "'Ah, stubborn children,' declares the LORD, 'who carry out a plan, but not mine.'" Distant from God, negligent of God's Word, it is no wonder that Rehoboam chose the path of folly that leads to ruin.

Rehoboam did not pray, did not seek wisdom in God's Word, did not even heed the advice of the elders; and in this way he brought himself and his cause to ruin.

Rehoboam's actions reveal the Bible's attitude toward the new versus the old. But we want to be careful not to press this matter too far, for the Bible does not advocate a mindless traditionalism. Not everything is better simply because it is older. Martyn Lloyd-Jones, preaching on this text, makes this observation:

> Slavishly to listen to that which is said merely because it is old is madness. Nothing can be so deadening and soul-destroying in its influence as traditionalism. But at the same time there is nothing which is quite as blind and so utterly foolish and unintelligent as to ignore the past entirely and to jettison everything that has been handed on by tradition simply because it comes on to us from the past. That a thing has been believed for centuries does not prove that it is true, but it certainly ought to cause us to think seriously and ponder long before we lightly throw it overboard. To Rehoboam the age of these [elders] and their wisdom and knowledge and experience and understanding was nothing. Indeed it told against them. They belonged to a past age, they were behind the times, their age alone proved that they were wrong and that they must be wrong.[1]

The old is not necessarily better. Humankind has fostered false myths and deadly lies for centuries, and we should not receive these merely on account of their longevity. Yet the attitude that rejects the old and tested simply because it is not novel and innovative is one that the Bible reproves for its lack of humility and wisdom.

It is not merely the old that is pitted against the new in this account.

Rehoboam rejected not just tradition but the counsel and commands of God's Word in Scripture, as we saw from Deuteronomy. We also see in his decision, then, a choice between the wisdom of God and the wisdom of the world, between the Bible and the thinking of the times. Lloyd-Jones sums this up, writing, "We also are confronted by two ways and two possibilities. On the one hand is the Bible way and on the other is the way preferred and advocated by contemporary opinion and modern thought."[2] That choice is ever before the people of God, and Rehoboam's precedent makes clear where the path of blessing lies or, on the other hand, where the path of unbelief and judgment from God might take us.

JEROBOAM'S "NEW" RELIGION

Rehoboam's loss was Jeroboam's gain. As the latter was crowned, the political dimensions of Israel were set in place for the centuries to come. The house of David retained the loyalty of the tribes of Judah and Benjamin, together making up the kingdom of Judah in the south. All ten of the other tribes combined to form the kingdom of Israel under Jeroboam. God made promises to this new king similar to those He had given to others, if only he would walk in His ways: "If you will listen to all that I command you, and will walk in my ways, and do what is right in my eyes by keeping my statutes and my commandments, as David my servant did, I will be with you and will build you a sure house, as I built for David, and I will give Israel to you" (1 Kings 11:38).

If only Jeroboam would put the Lord first, following the command to practice devotion to God and holiness before the world, his throne would be secure. But if, on the other hand, he put his throne first, scheming and striving in unbelief to retain what God had given him by grace, all would be lost. First Kings 12:26-27 tells us which course he chose: "And Jeroboam said in his heart, 'Now the kingdom will turn back to the house of David. If this people go up to offer sacrifices in the temple of the LORD at Jerusalem, then the heart of this people will turn again to their lord, to Rehoboam king of Judah, and they will kill me and return to Rehoboam king of Judah.'"

Jeroboam was intimidated by his rival's famous bloodline. He especially felt insecure because the temple of the Lord, beautiful and spectacular as a true artistic and spiritual wonder, the site where God commanded the people to go to worship Him, was in the city that Rehoboam still controlled. Jeroboam's solution to this problem made him a paragon for all those who for fear of losing end up destroying all. His plan was as odious as it was rebellious against the Lord: "So the king took counsel and made two calves of gold. And he said to the people, 'You have gone up to Jerusalem long enough. Behold your gods, O Israel, who brought you up out of the land of Egypt.' And he set one in Bethel, and the other he put in Dan. Then this thing became a sin, for the people went as far as Dan to be before one" (vv. 28-30).

Committed to this dreadful course, Jeroboam put together his own shrines, his own priesthood, and his own festivals at which he himself made the sacrifices. Devotion to the Lord—the only thing that would make his throne secure—became a hindrance in Jeroboam's mind; so he turned his back on the Lord to establish his own loyal and national religion. The logic is straightforward enough. Had not the Lord given him a kingdom? Should not he take prudent steps to secure that kingdom and the loyalty of his people? If his innovations in religious practice served those laudable ends, then the ends justified the means, did they not? What were a bunch of old and worn-out commands compared to the demands of the moment—commands like the second commandment, in which God insisted, "You shall not make for yourself a carved image" (Exod. 20:4)? Furthermore, the people liked the visible and attractive and innovative in religion! This new idea would work. It would bring the crowds to his new shrines; it would keep them from disloyally going down to Jerusalem to worship with Rehoboam. You see how compelling this logic was—reasoning that is repeated today in an increasing number of evangelical churches—once he had simply unfettered himself from the old, that is, from the Word of God, the Scriptures.

And work it did! The northern tribes would never again worship in the old ways. What Jeroboam started as a religious innovation suited to the times, a reorganized faith "he had devised from his own heart" (1 Kings 12:33), would lead to a whole new spiritual era in Israel. Jereboam's new religion did indeed solidify the nation he had started, until God finally judged these idolatrous people with a destruction that removed them from the scene of history and further biblical revelation altogether.

So effective was Jeroboam's self-serving program of the new in religion that his nation ceased practicing biblical religion altogether. Not one king who followed him would be commended for his faithfulness to the old ways and the old God; not one would be commended for "walking in the ways of David, who obeyed the Lord." In a very real way, the story of deformation in this northern kingdom ends with Jeroboam, for he introduced an entirely different religion that went beyond the bounds of mere deformation and into the realm of apostasy.

And yet we must notice that Jeroboam's innovations were really not new at all. This was simply an old but different faith, the pagan way of outward forms in the place of inward reality. It was the religious apparatus of idolatry, that which replaces God's grace with man's machinery, with the program of ritual and glitter that impresses man but offends God. Jeroboam's new idea was something quite old—golden calves! These were the very gods for which Israel was judged at Mount Sinai (Exod. 32). Here was a false transcendence in the place of the holy Lord, graven idols in their golden glory; here was a false imminence, a false closeness, in the calves' visible accessibility compared to the invisible but spiritual God of their fathers. Here was a religion they could control, a self-serving spirituality. Yet, as is ever true of idolatry, it was they who became enslaved by their sin. As Solomon himself declared, there really is nothing new in religion, for "what has been is what will be, and what has been done is what will be done, and there is nothing new under the sun" (Eccl. 1:9). How many of our modern religious innovations are thus exposed, even as they condemn themselves in partaking of the spirit of Jeroboam's religion!

Therefore the choice is never really between the old and the new, for the new is merely a disguise for a different, older way, "a way that seems right to a man, but its end is the way to death" (Prov. 14:12). The choice is between present and apparent success, as defined by ourselves, versus fidelity to the God of the Bible, the living God who both defines and provides blessing to those who trust in Him. Threatened by the brilliance and glory of Solomon's temple on Mount Zion, Jeroboam constructed his own religion of visible glory. But it could never provide the security and prosperity he craved, for idols never serve but always enslave. In epic and tragic folly, Jeroboam capitalized on the people's penchant for idolatry and established a pagan religion like that of the nations, betraying God for the sake of his own cause. Russell Dilday comments on this episode: "He was guilty of redesigning the faith for his own personal ends. . . . A religion of convenience, devised in one's own heart, is an abomination to God and is condemned by history as was the substitute faith of Jeroboam."[3]

Sadly, the Jeroboams are ever with us, justifying their supposedly new means with their own self-serving ends. Indeed, how many kings of our modern religious empires are truly heirs of Jeroboam! Yet they offer nothing new, but merely the old and weatherworn religion of the world, offering a tangible appeal while forging chains upon the souls of those who bow before their calves of gold.

A religion of convenience, redesigned for one's own personal ends, is an abomination to God and is condemned by history.

THE MAN OF GOD AND THE WORD OF GOD

At this point one known simply as "a man of God . . . out of Judah" (1 Kings 13:1) enters the scene. This unnamed prophet was sent to confront Jeroboam at Bethel, to deliver the Lord's condemnation on the false religion the king had set up there. The monarch, standing over the altar, "stretched out his hand from the altar, saying, 'Seize him!'" But the hand he stretched out toward the man shriveled up (v. 4). Such is the weakness of idolatry against the true power of God! At Jeroboam's request, the man of God prayed, and the king's arm was restored. Realizing that he was facing true divine power rather than the petty charade of his own religion, Jeroboam altered his approach, seeking to co-opt what he could not conquer. Here is a standard strategy of worldly religion, a phony peace in the interest of brotherhood and charity, a fatal alliance between the true and the false. Here before the golden calves of Bethel, an appropriate setting if ever there was one, Jeroboam proposed a prototype for many ecumenical gatherings yet to come: "The king said to the man of God, 'Come home with me, and refresh yourself, and I will give you a reward'" (v. 7).

The man of God rejected this poisoned palm branch, showing himself willing to be separate from the idolater in order to be faithful to God. In his reply to the king, he sets an example for us by taking his direction from the Word of God he had received by revelation. It is by taking our stand upon God's Word, he shows us, that we are enabled to resist the charms and threats of the world.

And the man of God said to the king, "If you give me half your house, I will not go in with you. And I will not eat bread or drink water in this place, for so was it commanded me by the word of the LORD, saying, 'You shall neither eat bread nor drink water nor return by the way that you came.'" So he went another way and did not return by the way that he came to Bethel.

—vv. 8-10

This man of God from Judah had received a revelation from God, and he was determined to obey it. So far, so good. But the story takes another twist that gets interesting when a different prophet, one from nearby Bethel, heard about this man of God from Judah and set out to meet him. This new angle in the story, one with an important point to make, picks up in verse 14, where the prophet from Bethel encounters the prophet from Judah:

And he went after the man of God and found him sitting under an oak. And he said to him, "Are you the man of God who came from Judah?" And he said, "I am." Then he said to him, "Come home with me and eat bread." And he said, "I may not return with you, or go in with you, neither will I eat bread nor drink water with you in this place, for it was said to me by the word of the LORD, 'You shall neither eat bread nor drink water there, nor return by the way that you came.'" And he said to him, "I also am a prophet as you are, and an angel spoke to me by the word of the LORD, saying, 'Bring him back with you into your house that he may eat bread and drink water.'" But he lied to him.

—vv. 14-18

Things had gotten complicated, as they often do. The man of God had received a revelation from God, and now this man, claiming also to be a prophet, tells him that he has a new word from God given through an angel. How is the prophet from Judah to handle this? The story concludes:

So he went back with him and ate bread in his house and drank water. And as they sat at the table, the word of the LORD came to the prophet who had brought him back. And he cried to the man of God who came from Judah, "Thus says the LORD,

'Because you have disobeyed the word of the LORD and have not kept the command that the LORD your God commanded you, but have come back and have eaten bread and drunk water in the place of which he said to you, "Eat no bread and drink no water," your body shall not come to the tomb of your fathers.'" And after he had eaten bread and drunk, he saddled the donkey for the prophet whom he had brought back. And as he went away a lion met him on the road and killed him. And his body was thrown in the road, and the donkey stood beside it; the lion also stood beside the body.

—VV. 19-24

Here is this poor prophet. He has served God courageously and well. He has stood up to the wicked king and has waged war in the power of the Lord. He has refused to be deterred from his path, has withstood the temptation to be co-opted by the king, and has gone the way God had told him. Then along comes this man also claiming to be a prophet and asserting a claim to divine warrant. He speaks of an easier way, claiming that an angel had told him the first prophet could rest and relax. The point is, this contradicts the earlier revelation the man of God had received from God. And for listening to this new and contradictory word, the faithful man of God is struck down by the Lord.

What was this man's terrible crime? He erred by failing to test the word of a prophet, as prescribed in God's commands in Deuteronomy. There we are told that God allows false prophets with enticing messages: "The LORD your God is testing you, to know whether you love the LORD your God with all your heart and with all your soul" (13:3). We need to pay attention to this, because this man received a purported word from the Lord that contradicted prior revelation from God. In forming His people, God had anticipated this very situation, giving the commands we have seen in the book of Deuteronomy. False prophecy is to be condemned, even if accompanied by miracles, even if given by the mouth of an angel. We see now what the apostle Paul was getting at when he wrote to the Galatians:

But even if we or an angel from heaven should preach to you a gospel contrary to the one we preached to you, let him be accursed. As we have said before, so now I say again: If anyone

is preaching to you a gospel contrary to the one you received,
let him be accursed.

—GAL. 1:8-9

But we love novelty in theology, we love a new word from the Lord, particularly when it tells us what we already want to do and believe. Perhaps this too was the man's weakness. Why was he so ready to believe this false prophecy? Perhaps because it was exactly what he was hoping to hear. He was hungry, and he was tired, and here was an opportunity to let down his guard.

So, too, is ours a time that embraces new words, new theologies, new formulations. We hear this all the time today: "We need to get away from the old, puritanical, restrictive way of looking at things . . . We need a new approach that fits the new way of things." The new is seen as better. "New Generation Detergent" is a better cleanser than the old detergent; new model cars are more desirable than the old junkers; new computers are faster than the old obsolete model that came out last month. Surely, as well, new approaches to spiritual matters are better than the stuffy old Gospel, the boring old-style Bible Christianity that was the rock of our fathers.

If we are not as bad as Rehoboam, arrogantly looking down on the old in favor of what is current and in vogue, we are often like Jeroboam, glad and excited to be free of the inhibitions from the "irrelevant" and "outdated" teachings of the Bible. If that is too strong a description, it is surely true that we are very often like this man of God from Judah: We lazily and unfaithfully use some excuse to believe new and attractive words without testing them against the old and reliable and God-revealed Word of the Bible. Surely there is a great difference between this man of God and the two unbelieving kings. Yet his faithlessness did not go unpunished, just as theirs would lead to death.

We love novelty in theology; we love a new word from the
Lord, particularly when it tells us what we already want to do.
But all new light must correspond with the old light or else it
is not light at all, but merely darkness masquerading as light.

The test the prophet failed is one that always confronts the people of God. A popular phrase today is: "We believe that God has fresh light to break forth from the Scriptures." That is almost the motto of our time. You see that phrase in magazines and as a header in academic catalogs. It is true, of course, that the Scriptures are not done speaking to us, that new things are yet to be learned from the Bible. There is a right and proper and exciting call to Christian scholarship, with much to be gleaned and taught to the glory of God. And yet there is a great danger in this kind of statement. Those who emphasize this new light from Scripture seldom seem to mention the Deuteronomic principle of testing prophecy—that all new light must correspond with the old light or else it is not light at all, but darkness masquerading as light, even as Satan loves to masquerade as an angel of light.

Again, we often hear the famous quote, "All truth is God's truth." How can a statement like that be refuted? All truth is God's truth, but all *claims* to truth are not God's truth. The prophet from Bethel was not speaking God's truth, though he claimed to be. I find that this saying tends mainly to be used to support the validity of nonbiblical sources. People say "all truth is God's truth" when they want us to buy into secular psychology or New Age practice, philosophic forms or the latest interpretive method arising from critical scholarship.

All truth is God's truth, but all claims to truth are not God's truth. The Bible alone is the very Word of God, the God-breathed Scriptures that are distinctive in providing us inerrant revelation from God. No other source bears this credential.

All truth may be God's truth, but let us not forget that the Bible alone is the very Word of God, the God-breathed Scriptures that are distinctive in providing us with inerrant revelation from God. No other source bears this credential and binds the conscience with this authority. Failure to remember this will surely have us believing claims to truth that are not truth, will have us sitting down at tables with prophets like that nice gentleman from Bethel, who speak words of death into our unsuspecting but unfaithful ears.

What a contemporary figure is this man of God from Judah! We can hardly find a better portrait of the evangelical movement today. He had been courageous in serving the Lord, just as evangelicals have been courageous in opposing an unbelieving culture. He had refused to be swayed by voices seeking to lead him astray, both as they threatened and as they sweetly cajoled, just as evangelicals avoided so much of the deadly siren songs of the secular twentieth century. Perhaps he was thinking about what a great servant he had been, in the very way we as evangelicals have smugly patted ourselves on the back; perhaps he was newly confident in his own ability to live out the godly life. Yet when a message from one who wore the garb of a friend came to him, even a message that flatly contradicted the Word of God he had received, this man of God was easily overtaken and destroyed. So also is the evangelical movement today being ruined by its willingness to hear and follow patently unbiblical methods and claims to truth simply because they were heard on Christian radio or sold in a Christian bookstore or hawked by a man sporting a fish symbol on his automobile bumper.

The evangelical movement today is being destroyed by its willingness to follow patently unbiblical methods and claims to truth simply because they were heard on Christian radio or sold in a Christian bookstore.

For both this sorry man of God in the record of 1 Kings and the evangelicals of our day, a willingness to listen to the new even when it runs counter to the old (the Word of God) is a recipe for disaster and even for death. In His letter to the churches in Revelation, our exalted Lord condemns those churches that tolerate false teaching, commending those that "tested those who call themselves apostles and are not, and found them to be false" (Rev. 2:2). The love of novelty and the threat of false claims to truth constantly stalk the church, gravely threatening her with deformation and consequent judgment. Jesus therefore commands, "Remember, then, what you received and heard. Keep it, and repent" (Rev. 3:3). Against the threat of deformation, our Lord Himself sounds the call for reformation, a return to truth through watchful commitment to God's revealed Word.

5

THE KING AT THE CROSSROADS

As the record of Israel's up-and-down, mostly down, progress continues in the books of Kings, the individual accounts become much briefer. The purpose is not to chronicle the details of every regime, but rather to depict the trend and pattern revealed by the infidelity of successive generations. Meanwhile, as 1 and 2 Kings move inexorably toward the destruction of Jerusalem in 586 B.C., the portrait of deformation picks up new scenes and new dimensions for our benefit.

After the biblical record of the calamities of Rehoboam and Jeroboam, much of 1 and 2 Kings deals with the great problem that arose from the house of Omri (ruled 880-874 B.C.) and especially during the reign of his wicked son Ahab (ruled 874-853 B.C.), who established Samaria as a strong capital for the northern kingdom of Israel. Their dynasty so opposed the Lord and the biblical faith that under these kings the northern kingdom left the realm of mere deformation for outright apostasy into pagan idolatry. In secular terms Omri and Ahab seem to have been effective and powerful rulers. As such they posed a grave threat to the house of David in Judah. So serious was this threat that God raised up to oppose them a man who was arguably the greatest of all the prophets, Elijah the Tishbite (1 Kings 17—2 Kings 2).

During Ahab's reign Judah was ruled by one of the true heroes of the Old Testament, Jehoshaphat (ruled 872-848 B.C.), whom we will later consider as a great reformation leader. In the years that followed, however, both the kings of the north and south were disobedient to the Lord, with only a few examples of fidelity among the kings of Judah. By the time King Ahaz assumed the throne of Judah in 732 B.C. the old hostility between north and south was deeply entrenched. So hostile, in fact, was Israel to the southern kingdom that it entered into an alliance with the neighboring nation of Syria against Judah. Israel's main concern was to oppose the mounting power of the Assyrian Empire in the north; apparently the main objective against Judah was to secure the rear in order to concentrate on the northern front. After a number of victories against Judah, this northern alliance sputtered out and fell short of the goal of capturing Jerusalem. Still, a serious threat faced Ahaz that would define his reign as king.

A CONFERENCE AT THE CROSSROADS

As in the case of Elijah, the gravity of this situation is measured by the stature of the man God sent to deal with it. In response to this crisis another great prophet, Isaiah son of Amoz, arrives on the scene. The seventh chapter of Isaiah tells the story of his dealings with this king, along with additional information provided in 2 Kings 16 and 2 Chronicles 28:

> *When the house of David was told, "Syria is in league with Ephraim," the heart of Ahaz and the heart of his people shook as the trees of the forest shake before the wind. And the LORD said to Isaiah, "Go out to meet Ahaz, you and Shear-jashub your son, at the end of the conduit of the upper pool on the highway to the Washer's Field."*
>
> —ISA. 7:2-3

Upon that fateful ground, the crossroads outside Jerusalem, the king and his advisers were gathered, probably to view the front lines from a forward vantage point, or perhaps to inspect the security of the vital water supply. As the party was discussing diplomatic and military matters, up came the representative of the realm they had so far ignored, the spiritual realm. The Lord had sent His prophet with a message for the king, one of assurance but also one with sober repercussions. Isaiah faithfully delivered the message:

> *"Say to him, 'Be careful, be quiet, do not fear, and do not let your heart be faint because of these two smoldering stumps of firebrands, at the fierce anger of Rezin and Syria and the son of Remaliah. Because Syria, with Ephraim and the son of*

> *Remaliah [Pekah, Israel's king], has devised evil against you,*
> *saying, "Let us go up against Judah and terrify it, and let us con-*
> *quer it for ourselves, and set up the son of Tabeel as king in the*
> *midst of it,"' thus says the* LORD *God: 'It shall not stand, and*
> *it shall not come to pass. . . . [But] if you are not firm in faith,*
> *you will not be firm at all.'"*
>
> —ISA. 7:4-9

The point is clear. Judah lacked the military strength to withstand the enemy coalition; but what the king and his people lacked, the Lord possessed in abundance. God described the kings who so terrified Ahaz and his counselors as mere "smoldering stumps of firebrands," which may indicate that their strength was spent, their fire near to burning out. The way the prophet goes on to belittle Judah's enemies seems strange: "The head of Syria is Damascus, and the head of Damascus is Rezin. . . . And the head of Ephraim is Samaria, and the head of Samaria is the son of Remaliah" (vv. 8-9). Probably this is meant to emphasize the houses from which these kings arose and the cities from which they reigned. If so, there is an obvious though unstated contrast with Ahaz and his house and city. Rezin was the son of Tabeel, and his city was Damascus. Pekah was the son of Remaliah, from the city of Ephraim, that is, Samaria. The point is not their strength but their weakness, as specified by the added prophecy, later fulfilled by the Assyrian conquest and deportation of the northern kingdom: "Within sixty-five years Ephraim will be broken to pieces so that it will no longer be a people" (v. 8).

Such was the power of those arrayed against Judah, such were their houses and their cities. What then of Ahaz? Was he not of the house of David, the man after God's heart, to whom divine promises of an eternal throne had been made? The house of David claimed God Himself as its sword and shield! And from what city did Ahaz rule? Was it not Jerusalem, the city of God, of which the psalmist sang, "God is within her, she will not fall; God will help her at break of day" (Ps. 46:5, NIV). Therefore Ahaz was to remember the Lord, to remember His promises and power; he was to repent of his schemes and turn to God in faith. If he did this, explains J. Alec Motyer, "The Lord could be trusted to keep his promises to David and to deal with the threat. . . . The issue was as clear cut as that: will Ahaz seek salvation by works (politics, alliances) or by simple trust in divine promises?"[1]

A REVEALING CHOICE

In our study of Deuteronomy we noted the foundational principle of salvation by grace alone. This doctrine, which we normally apply to individual salvation, has corporate implications as well. Specifically, God's people can rely on His gracious power for their deliverance. Thus we read Moses' exhortation on the fields of Moab: "Do not fear or panic or be in dread of them, for the LORD your God is he who goes with you to fight for you against your enemies, to give you the victory" (Deut. 20:3-4). This is the message Isaiah brought to Ahaz, a message that was more astonishing still because the king had hardly been a model of faith. Nonetheless, here at the end of his resources, in danger of losing his life and his throne, God's messenger came to Ahaz with an offer of deliverance if only he would trust himself to the Lord.

Salvation by grace alone has corporate as well as individual implications. God's people can rely on His gracious power for their deliverance. God's messenger came to Ahaz with an offer of deliverance if only he would trust himself to the Lord.

Sadly, in his own mind Ahaz had not yet reached the end of his resources. Militarily he was outmatched, but there was one more card he could play before he would have to bend the knee to the Lord and submit to the word of the prophet. This was the diplomatic card— namely, the idea of appealing to one of the great powers of the day for aid against his enemies. If Israel and Ammon together posed a vastly superior threat to Judah, there was always Assyria, to the north of those kingdoms, which was vastly superior to them. To put it in terms of a child's game, if Israel and Ammon were scissors to Judah's paper, Assyria was the rock that could break the scissors in two.

At this time in history, Assyria was the dominant power in the ancient world. Its current ruler, Tiglath-Pileser III (ruled 745-727 B.C.), had considerably extended his territory in the direction of the Middle East and would be only too glad to gain a pretext for more extensive intervention in the region. The cost for his aid would be steep: Assyria would insist upon a paternal control over the affairs of Judah, making Jerusalem a vassal territory to pagan powers. Furthermore, Ahaz would have to bow before and make offerings to the gods of Assyria, opening further inroads to idolatry in the life of God's people.

Isaiah offered a different way. Ahaz could call upon the name of the Lord, the God of Israel who had made such great promises to the house of David. Whether the king had forgotten or had never really learned this, Isaiah informed him that he need not bow to the powers of this world, he need not sell his soul and his future to avoid the disaster that loomed on the horizon. Indeed, trusting himself to a nation like Assyria and giving himself to its false gods would ultimately prove his undoing. This comes across in dire terms in verses 8-9. A clear parallelism links their endings: "Within sixty-five years Ephraim will be broken to pieces. . . . If you are not firm in faith, you will not be firm at all." In other words, if Judah followed Israel's example of unbelief, the destruction prophesied of the northern kingdom would become the fate of the southern kingdom as well. In this way Isaiah's call to faith included a warning of judgment if Judah did not heed that call.

One of the great themes of the book of Isaiah is a denunciation of idols and idolatry. Later in his prophecy, Isaiah depicts the destruction that awaits idols and all who trust in them: "The images that are carried about are burdensome, a burden for the weary. They stoop and bow down together; unable to rescue the burden, they themselves go off into captivity." The idols, he says, are a burden to those who serve them. Having no strength, they must be borne on the backs of their worshipers; having no life of their own, they consume the lives of those who follow after them. But in contrast the true God, the God of the Bible, can say of Himself: "I am he who will sustain you. I have made you and I will carry you; I will sustain you and I will rescue you" (Isa. 46:1-4, NIV).

Most of us can remember the fall of the Soviet Union and seeing pictures of the Lenin statues lying on their sides, the head severed or perhaps an arm broken off. What was the picture? The old order had crumbled, but there was more: The whole system in which that people trusted, that they gloried in, was shown to be feeble, pathetic, utterly ruinous. The Soviet Union and its mystique were very much like Assyria and her gods. Great though they appeared in the day of their power, the broken gods ultimately showed themselves weak and useless to those who served them.

This is how Christians should reflect on the trial in which King Ahaz found himself. It was a testing of his faith, of his fidelity to God, of his practical theology. So, too, are our trials, individually or together in the church, tests of faith. When the gods of the world seem ascendant, when it seems that the old way, the stuffy conservative way of the Bible, is a losing strategy, when counselors and consultants assure us the only way to beat them is to join them, God is testing our faith. God Himself is not under trial—He never really is—and history shows that the greatest of empires are but tools in His hand for the testing of the church, tools He raises up and casts aside at His will.

What threats concern the church today? What worldly powers prey upon our sense of security, as his northern enemies preyed upon the peace of King Ahaz? We might identify an eroding moral climate or a godless government agenda. We might think of the intellectual influence of secular humanism, with its values of relativism and materialism that parade before the church like the armies of Damascus and Samaria. There is increasing government intolerance for religious expression, a betrayal in the courts of our constitutional heritage of free speech. These are just a few of the very real threats that Christians must ponder today. Just as in Isaiah's day, it is a challenge to know how to respond. Like King Ahaz, church leaders must choose a course of action.

What should we do in these troubling times? According to many, what we need today are new alliances. Some say, openly or not, that the church must join forces with Hollywood. We must employ entertainment strategies to lure people into what used to be called a sanctuary but now is called an auditorium, to persuade them it is more fun and fulfilling to be a Christian than to be an unbeliever. But is this any different from Ahaz's unholy alliance? According to others, we must make an alliance with Washington, pushing back our enemies with muscles of our own in terms they will respect, counterattacking godlessness with the aid of political Tiglath-Pilesers and media Pharaohs. But is this different in principle from the logic of Ahaz? Are there any who look to God as sufficient in His grace for the trials of His people?

Thankfully, God has not left us without instruction, without a plan to follow. He says that we should do nothing—nothing, that is, but trust ourselves to Him while we go about our worship and service to Him. We are to hold fast to what the Bible teaches, to what we saw in the book of Deuteronomy: exclusive devotion to the Lord, holiness before the world, salvation by grace alone, trust in God's sufficient Word, and a positive program of justice and mercy. That is what we are to do—remain the church, remain God's people, the ark of peace in the storm of this world.

That is precisely what God commands of us, just as Isaiah counseled Ahaz the King to "Be careful, be quiet, do not fear, and do not let your heart be faint" (Isa. 7:4). God assures us that our foes will not long stand, just as Ephraim would soon go into exile (v. 8). God warns us, as he did the king at the crossroads long before, "If you do not stand firm in your faith, you will not stand at all" (v. 9, NIV).

Lest we think this an isolated example, wrongly generalized and applied to our situation, we need only consider the many other instances when God gave this same instruction to His people in danger. What did God say to Moses when Israel's back was to the Red Sea? "Fear not, stand firm, and see the salvation of the LORD, which he will work for you today. . . . The LORD will fight for you, and you have only to be silent" (Exod. 14:13-14). What were Joshua's instructions when he undertook the daunting task of replacing Moses and leading the people against the nations of Canaan? "I will be with you. I will not leave you or forsake you. . . . Only be strong and very courageous, being careful to do according to all the law that Moses my servant commanded you. Do not turn from it to the right hand or to the left, that you may have good success wherever you go. . . . Do not be frightened, and do not be dismayed, for the LORD your God is with you wherever you go" (Josh. 1:5-9). God said the same to faithful Jehoshaphat in the face of yet another deadly threat: "Do not be afraid and do not be dismayed at this great horde, for the battle is not yours but God's. . . . Stand firm, hold your position, and see the salvation of the LORD on your behalf" (2 Chron. 20:15-17). Surely this is a message for every group of Christians, every struggling church, beleaguered by the forces of this world, by danger, by failure, by weary discouragement and loss: "Do not be afraid; do not be discouraged. The Lord will be with you."

All of this presupposes two essential facts, facts Isaiah pressed upon King Ahaz: namely, that God was *able* to defend Jerusalem from the threats posed against her and also that He was *willing* to do so. The whole thrust of the prophet's message assured King Ahaz of both these truths, if only he would trust the Lord. But Ahaz refused. Instead, he turned to Assyria's king as one who was able to help him and who would be willing to do so for a price Ahaz was willing to pay. There always is a price to pay for alliances with the world, a world intolerant of fidelity to God and especially of holiness among God's people. Ahaz's price was to enter into binding covenant with Assyria—in place of his covenant with God—including the recognition of Assyria's gods and an admission of their supremacy.

Second Kings 16:10-16 tells the terrible tale of Ahaz's journey to meet the Assyrian king, Tiglath-Pileser, during which Ahaz agreed to rearrange the temple of the Lord in Jerusalem according to the pattern of the pagan Assyrian worship. From the standpoint of Deuteronomy, a more horrible scene could hardly be imagined: "He saw the altar that was at Damascus. And King Ahaz sent to Uriah the priest a model of the altar, and its pattern, exact in all its details. And Uriah the priest built the altar; in accordance with all that King Ahaz had sent from Damascus . . ." (2 Kings 16:11-12). All of this was done, we are told, "because of the king of Assyria" (v. 18).

Whenever God's people forget that salvation is by grace from an all-powerful God, who is willing and able to meet all of our needs and to protect us from all of our foes, the inevitable result is an alliance with the world that proves costly through betrayal of the Lord.

What a chilling foretaste of scenes so common in our day—the rearrangement of the church sanctuary to fit the agenda of the gods of entertainment with whom we have allied, the sanctuary renamed the auditorium, the chancel replaced with the stage, the pulpit removed, the Scripture reading or congregational prayer jettisoned for drama or even sacred dance. In this way, pagan religion often enters the church as powerfully, though not as obviously, as when Ahaz set up the idols in the temple on Mt. Zion. Another unholy alliance has evangelical leaders receiving marching orders from Washington and crafting sermon points for the sake of the power games of the nation. Whenever God's people forget that salvation is by grace from an all-powerful God who is willing and able to meet all of our needs, to protect us from all of our foes, the inevitable result is an alliance with the world that proves costly through betrayal of the Lord. What choice do we have, people will say, their eyes fixed not on God in His power but on the powers arrayed against us in the world? We face the same choice given to the king at the crossroads: whether or not to receive and keep the pattern of worship and service laid down by God in the Bible, looking to Him and relying on His power and ever-faithful love.

God gives us a choice; indeed, it is always this choice that more than any other defines a given age. In our choice of the invisible God or the visible powers of the world, we reveal not merely our *professed* theology but also our *practiced* theology. If we believe truly in the God of the Bible, the one who is mighty to save, then that choice will bear out in what we do and in the weapons we wield. The apostle Paul, speaking to another generation in difficult straits, set forth in practical terms what it means to trust God: "For though we walk in the flesh, we are not waging war according to the flesh. For the weapons of our warfare are not of the flesh but have divine power to destroy strongholds. We destroy arguments and every lofty opinion raised against the knowledge of God, and take every thought captive to obey Christ" (2 Cor. 10:3-5).

A SIGN FROM THE LORD

How discouraging Ahaz's unbelief must have been to the prophet, but Isaiah did not give up easily. Starting in Isaiah 7:10 we read of a sign he offered to strengthen the king's faltering faith. It is not clear whether this took place at the time of the earlier message or sometime later. What is clear is that Ahaz was granted a rare privilege of receiving from God a sign to prove that His promise of protection was true. The singular character of this offer suggests the significance of this chapter in the history of God's people. This remarkable episode is reported in Isaiah 7:10-12:

> *Again the LORD spoke to Ahaz, "Ask a sign of the LORD your God; let it be deep as Sheol or high as heaven." But Ahaz said, "I will not ask, and I will not put the LORD to the test."*

It is one thing to demand a sign from God because of unbelief, which is a great sin. But it is another to have God offer such a sign as an incentive to grow into a stronger faith. In the latter case, to refuse the sign is to sin, deliberately to choose unbelief, to refuse what is helpful to faith in the Lord. How well this reveals Ahaz's heart; here was not a weak believer doing his best to understand, but a hardened rebel who deliberately rejected God's help and salvation. When the king refused, Isaiah declared that Ahaz would nevertheless receive God's sign. Isaiah's next statement is one of the most remarkable assertions in the Bible: "Hear then, O house of David! Is it too little for you to weary men, that you weary my God also? Therefore the Lord himself will give you a sign. Behold, the virgin shall conceive and bear a son, and shall call his name Immanuel" (vv. 13-14).

Vast reservoirs of ink have been spilled explaining or denying how the virgin birth of Jesus Christ served as a sign to unbelieving Ahaz (Matthew 1:22-23 states plainly that it was Jesus' virgin birth that the prophet predicted). But I think we have merely to ask how the king would have responded were he among the shepherds that first Christmas in Bethlehem's stable. What would have run through Ahaz's mind had he gazed upon the little baby swaddled in a manger? I think he would have been thoroughly unimpressed. "This is what is supposed to make me trust the Lord—a baby born in such poor circumstances, in weakness and humiliation? You expect this to make me turn from the legions of chariots and chests filled with gold that Assyria brings to the table?" Can there be any doubt that Ahaz's response to the virgin-born child would have gone something like "What kind of sign is this at a time of national disaster!"

But the virgin birth of Christ is a sign to every generation, to those before but especially to those after His miraculous and humble entry into the world. But of what is it a sign? The virgin birth is a sign of salvation by grace alone.

Compare the virgin birth with its Old Testament counterpart, the child born from the barren womb. God had promised Abraham a son who would carry on his name and fulfill the aims of the covenant. And yet his wife Sarah was old and barren. Abraham, not trusting the Lord, took matters into his own hands, taking Sarah's maid, Hagar, and having a son through her. But in Genesis 18 the angels appeared to tell him that God would give life to Sarah's womb, that God would give him a legitimate child through his ninety-year-old wife. The message was to trust God in the place of human failure and human frustration, and not to take matters into our own hands. It was through Isaac, this child of promise, God's gift of grace, and not through Ishmael, the child of unbelief and human works, that God would bring his blessing.

*God would give a child through Abraham's ninety-year-old,
barren wife. The message here was to trust God in the place of
human failure and human frustration, and not to take matters
into our own hands.*

Later, in the time of the judges, an angel came to a man named
Manoah, announcing that his barren wife would give birth to a deliverer named Samson. Again, a few years later, God answered the heart-
broken prayers of the barren woman Hannah, who pleaded to give birth
to a son. That child was Samuel, the great judge and prophet and deliverer of Israel from the Philistines.

You see the connection. In Old Testament times God sent cham-
pions who would deliver the people from human enemies, and He
often brought these deliverers through a barren womb to show that
salvation is by grace alone, not through human effort. Seeing God
bring a child in this way taught the people not to trust human wisdom
and human effort, not to despair in the face of human failure, but
rather to trust God who gives life to the dead and produces deliverance from the barren womb. He is, as Paul writes in Romans 4, "the
God. . . . who gives life to the dead and calls into existence the things
that do not exist" (v. 17).

But, of course, there is a very great difference when it comes to the
birth of Jesus Christ. Here God sends the promised deliverer who will
save the people not from the Philistines, not from Samaria and Syria, but
from their sins. And God sends Him through a womb that is not merely
barren but virgin. Before, God showed the sufficiency of His power in
the place of human futility and failure; here we have a case where human
effort is not even in view, is not even an appropriate category for the task
at hand. Here is not a field that has been planted in vain, but a field on
which no plow has been laid. Here is a creation by the Spirit of God
alone, where the will of man would not dare to tread. The virgin birth
provides a towering sign of a God who saves by His grace and power
alone. Surely this message applies to every group of Christians, every
struggling church, beleaguered by the forces of this world, by danger, by
failure, by weary discouragement and loss.

What does this proclaim to us but that God's church may depend
on this grace that can do what we cannot? What does it say about the

work of the church, but that it bears its fruit from Sarah's womb and not from Hagar's? Ours is a salvation that can only succeed if a virgin girl gives birth to a son. On what basis will we then ally ourselves to the Assyrias of this world, worship their gods of money and power and prestige, or employ their methods of persuasion and compulsion and enticement? In the starkest possible contrast to the choice of men like Ahaz, we are called to serve at an altar whose stones were not hewn by human hands; we serve a kingdom that comes crashing into the kingdoms of this world with heavenly power, a rock "cut from a mountain by no human hand" (Dan. 2:45).

The gospel ministry is one that bears its fruit from Sarah's womb and not from Hagar's. It is one that can only succeed if a virgin girl gives birth to a son.

If ever a man trusted himself to God alone, that man was Jesus Christ. And if ever a test tried the soul, that test was the cross He bore. Like Ahaz, Jesus faced His day of testing. We read of it in the Gospel accounts of the Garden of Gethsemane. His soul overwhelmed with sorrow, His heart burdened with the weight of what lay ahead, Jesus did what Ahaz would not do—He prayed to His heavenly father. "My Father," he cried, anguished sweat beading on his brow, "if it be possible, let this cup pass from me; nevertheless, not as I will, but as you will" (Matt. 26:39).

Might Jesus have appealed to the powers of this world? The accounts of His arrest make it clear that He could have done better than that. Even when Peter drew forth a sword, that symbol of human might, Jesus turned back his hand, saying, "Do you think that I cannot appeal to my Father, and he will at once send me more than twelve legions of angels?" (Matt. 26:53). Jesus faced not danger but death, even the hell of God's wrath for our sins. Was there ever a strategy more weak, more foolish, more certain of failure as reckoned by this world? But Jesus accepted all of this with faith in God, rather than having legions of angels at His side while denying the will of His heavenly Father. The question, then, is this: Was He defeated, having accepted death and even hell? The answer is the open tomb of His resurrection and His subsequent exaltation to the right hand of God.

If ever a man trusted himself to God alone, that man was Jesus Christ at the cross. There was never a strategy more weak, more foolish, more certain of failure as reckoned by this world, but Jesus accepted all of this with faith in God.

If Isaiah gave to Ahaz the virgin birth as the sign of God's saving grace, our Lord Jesus gives to us the sign of His cross. When the crowds beckoned Him to the path of earthly glory and power, Jesus chose instead the cross. He said, "The Son of Man is about to be delivered into the hands of men" (Luke 9:44). That was His answer to the dangers and trials of His life. The cross is His sign for all who fear, who suffer, who sorrow at the hands of an evil world. It is a sign of God's sufficiency even in the death of His beloved Son, a sign that points to an open tomb where the light of resurrection shines. The cross of Christ, where Jesus conquered sin and death, is the sign, Paul says, of God's "incomparably great power for us who believe . . . like the working of his mighty strength, which he exerted in Christ when he raised him from the dead" (Eph. 1:19-20, NIV).

The power that comes through the cross is the power of God and not of man. Therefore, for all of us who stand at the crossroads of danger or worry or doubt, with a choice to make—whom we will choose and trust—Jesus Christ presents the sign not merely of His birth but also of His death, both of which speak of saving grace for all who will believe.

For all who stand at the crossroads of danger or worry or doubt, Jesus Christ presents the sign not merely of His birth but also of His death, both of which speak of saving grace for all who will believe.

ONCE MORE AT THE CROSSROADS

Ahaz did not believe; he did not cry out to the Lord but rather to the Assyrian king. The result was disastrous. The pagan ruler came striking down, ultimately destroying Samaria and carting off the ten northern tribes of God's people, never to be heard from again. John Oswalt sums up the whole sordid episode: "Ahaz had an opportunity to trust God for deliverance. Instead he trusted Assyria, his worst enemy. The result, as Isaiah predicted, was that Assyria herself overran the land."[2] Ahaz may have taken satisfaction in this turn of events; yet it was a poisoned chalice from which he drank. Though he saved his life, he lost his soul; though he retained his seat, it was no longer the throne of a king.

This episode in deformation history has one more point to make, and it comes from the life of Ahaz's son and successor, Hezekiah. Hezekiah was a godly king who sought the Lord. "He did what was right in the eyes of the LORD, according to all that his father David had done" (2 Kings 18:3). This reformer king devoted himself to the removal of idols and the implementation of true worship of the Lord. During the early years of his reign the northern kingdom was invaded and destroyed. The Bible's own explanation is telling. All this happened "because they did not obey the voice of the LORD their God but transgressed his covenant, even all that Moses the servant of the Lord commanded" (2 Kings 18:12). God had formed His people through the words of Moses, but deformation had finally led to apostasy and from there to ultimate judgment and destruction.

This must have made a strong impression on Hezekiah, for he repudiated his father's alliance with Assyria, thus courting the wrath of this vastly superior power. Imagine how his father's old counselors would have gasped, if any remained in his service. Here was an abandonment of all earthly logic; yet it was a bold expression of faith in the power of God to save.

What is particularly fascinating is something that happened when Assyria invaded, under the new king Sennacherib. The enemy herald came and demanded the surrender of Jerusalem, and we read in Isaiah 36:

> *In the fourteenth year of King Hezekiah, Sennacherib king of Assyria came up against all the fortified cities of Judah and took them. And the king of Assyria sent the Rabshakeh from Lachish to King Hezekiah at Jerusalem, with a great army. And he stood by the conduit of the upper pool on the highway to the Washer's Field. And there came out to him Eliakim the son of Hilkiah, who was over the household, and Shebna the secretary, and Joah the son of Asaph, the recorder.*

—vv. 1-3

Note the precision in naming the place where this emissary stood; we can be sure that this detail is not merely mentioned in passing. The herald of the Assyrian king stood directly upon the ground where once

Jerusalem's king had stood. Ahaz and Isaiah had calmly carried on their political-theological debate safely outside the walls, along the road to the Washerman's Field by the aqueduct of the Upper Pool; now the new king stands back within the walls, behind the walls he so badly needs for protection. Where once his father stood with the prophet of the Lord now stands the prophet of godless opposition.

Here we see the retrograde principle of deformation in vivid display. This is what happens when God's people do not meet deformation head-on with repentance and reformation. They are pushed back step by step until finally they gaze meekly out from over their walls. The twentieth century gave a dazzling display of this principle. Early on many missionary agencies turned away from the Word of God. But Christians said, "It doesn't matter because the seminaries are strong." Before long the voice of unbelief began to call out from within the once-safe ivory towers. "That's all right," it was said, "because the pastors are sound." But it wasn't all that long before it was heard, "Even if the pastor speaks strange doctrines, the man in the pew is safe—we can count on him." How many pulpits, erected with the funds of godly Christians, now send forth denials of the faith! Where once spoke the prophet now speaks the mocking enemy of truth. Jesus told His disciples, "Watch and beware of the leaven of the Pharisees and Sadducees" (Matt. 16:6). For like yeast in bread, deformation soon spreads all through the loaf until the whole must be thrown out and cast aside. Hezekiah, faithfully seeking to restore the losses of his father's unbelief, gazed out from the walls to the place where his father had once stood, where the jeering voice of idolatry now called out.

Where once his father stood with the prophet of the Lord now stood the prophet of godless opposition. Such is the retrograde principle of deformation.

Hezekiah must have gazed from those walls bitterly lamenting his father's unbelief. And yet his position was not truly worse because of that earlier failure. In the final analysis his situation was precisely the same as that of Ahaz, precisely the same as that of every Christian in every trial. There is the world, advancing in its might, drawing nigh to the walls of God's city with mocking threats and scornful derision. And there in heaven is the God of glory, the Lord Almighty, by whose power the chariots of Pharaoh drowned in the sea. "The LORD is a man of war," Moses sang. "The LORD is his name. . . . The LORD will reign forever and ever" (Exod. 15:3, 18). Hezekiah's situation was not unique; failure to trust the Lord would lead him to ruin, while for him as well as for others God's promise would surely hold true: "Everyone who calls on the name of the LORD shall be saved" (Joel 2:32).

After Sennacherib's herald had taunted the inhabitants of the city, he placed a document with terms of surrender in the hands of Hezekiah's servants. They were terms his father would have recognized—only submit and worship our gods and you will be spared. But this king of Judah was animated by a different spirit, the Holy Spirit who grants repentance and faith. He tore his clothes and went to the temple, instructing all to pray to God for His help. Isaiah heard of this, and he sent a message from the Lord, a promise of victory and success.

Hezekiah took the letter from the Assyrian king and got down on his knees before the Lord in one of the great examples of true reformation. "O LORD our God," he prayed, "save us from his hand, that all the kingdoms of the earth may know that you alone are the LORD" (Isa. 37:20). That night "the angel of the LORD went out and struck down a hundred and eighty-five thousand in the camp of the Assyrians" (Isa. 37:36). Shocked by the power of God, Sennacherib retreated to Assyria, where soon he was killed by rivals to his throne.

Hezekiah's position was not truly worse because of the failure of his father. In the final analysis it was precisely the same as that of every Christian in every trial. There is the world, advancing in its might, and there in heaven is the God of glory, the Lord Almighty.

The apostle Paul writes of the Old Testament, "Now these things took place as examples for us, that we might not desire evil as they did" (1 Cor. 10:6). The writer of Hebrews, perhaps with Hezekiah in mind, speaks of those men of faith who "were made strong out of weakness, became mighty in war, put foreign armies to flight" (11:34). May the God who remains always the same grant us grace to profit from these examples, so that similar reports might be made in our times of "the victory that has overcome the world—our faith" (1 John 5:4).

6

THE VOICE OF THE PROPHET

The thoughtful reader will have noticed that our tale of deformation bears close relation to the principles we started with from Deuteronomy. It is the thesis of this book that God established definitive principles in the forming of His people and that deformation takes place when those principles are forgotten or abandoned. The choice of Saul as "a king to judge us like all the nations" (1 Sam. 8:5) was made by those no longer devoted to the Lord and who thus were unwilling to be holy in the world. That situation was reversed in the case of Solomon, who married the daughters of pagan nations and in so doing brought their gods into bed with them. Rehoboam and Jeroboam together bear testimony to the danger of that which is new and pleasing in the eyes and ears of men. The man of God from Judah's earthen grave warns against the new voice that contradicts the old word given by revelation from God. King Ahaz sought a human deliverance instead of the salvation from God that is by grace alone; the foolish king chose a salvation that was *of* the world, *by* the world, and ultimately sold him *to* the world as its slave and vassal.

Of the five principles highlighted from Deuteronomy, only that of social justice and mercy has escaped our notice. However, the record of faithless kings shows a nearly uniform transgression of this divine mandate. The prophet Isaiah makes this, along with idolatry, the main charge against his generation: "Your princes are rebels and companions of thieves. Everyone loves a bribe and runs after gifts. They do not bring justice to the fatherless, and the widow's cause does not come to them" (Isa. 1:23). As we turn in this chapter to study the time of Jeremiah, we find that false and hollow religion is especially exposed by its corruption and social injustice.

THE VOICE OF THE PROPHET

At every stage in deformation history, from Saul's coronation to Ahab's apostasy to Ahaz's foolish choice, Israel's leaders had forsaken God in the face of the prophets He sent to warn them and call them to reformation. This was God's own summary in the time of Jeremiah, which we have noted before: "I have sent to you all my servants the prophets, sending them persistently, saying, 'Turn now every one of you from his evil way, and amend your deeds, and do not go after other gods to serve them, and then you shall dwell in the land that I gave to you and your fathers.' But you did not incline your ear or listen to me" (Jer. 35:15). So also today and in every age, a telling sign of deformation is an unwillingness to hear and heed the prophetic voice of God's Word.

At every stage in deformation history, Israel's leaders had forsaken God in the face of the prophets He sent to warn them and call them back to reformation. A telling sign of deformation is an unwillingness to hear and heed the prophetic voice of God's Word.

We can find probably no better example of this than in the day of Jeremiah, who had the sad distinction of serving as God's prophet at the end of the trail of deformation in the Deuteronomic History. He was the weeping prophet whose eyes bore witness to the fall of blessed Jerusalem in flames and destruction. Jeremiah began his prophetic ministry in the time of Josiah, the great reformer king we will later consider, and continued to speak for God during the dark days that led to God's judgment under Josiah's sons.

Jerusalem heard Jeremiah's prophetic voice many times over a great many years, but one of the most significant occasions was his famous temple sermon, recorded in Jeremiah 7. Here he spoke out against the false religious institutionalism that surrounded the temple of the Lord on Mount Zion:

> *The word that came to Jeremiah from the LORD: "Stand in the gate of the LORD's house, and proclaim there this word, and say, Hear the word of the LORD, all you men of Judah who enter these gates to worship the LORD. Thus says the LORD of hosts, the God of Israel: Amend your ways and your*

*deeds, and I will let you dwell in this place. Do not trust in
these deceptive words: 'This is the temple of the* LORD, *the
temple of the* LORD, *the temple of the* LORD.' *For if you truly
amend your ways and your deeds, if you truly execute justice
one with another, if you do not oppress the sojourner, the
fatherless, or the widow, or shed innocent blood in this place,
and if you do not go after other gods to your own harm, then
I will let you dwell in this place, in the land that I gave of old
to your fathers forever. Behold, you trust in deceptive words
to no avail."*

—VV. 1-8

God sent Jeremiah to confront the religious institutionalism that
stood in the way of true worship of the Lord. This truly is a stunning
message, because it takes place at the temple that God Himself had
established for true religion, the dwelling-place where His *shekinah*
glory had once shone and where He had commanded the priests to make
offerings to Him.

What was wrong, then, with the people's chant, "The temple of the
LORD, the temple of the LORD, the temple of the LORD"? The problem
was that the people were trusting simply in their great religious heritage,
in the physical presence of the great temple, and because of this they gave
no attention to turning their hearts to the Lord. The temple had been
established to lead the people in worship of the Lord, not to be a substitute for God and for a living faith in Him. Philip G. Ryken describes
their false religion this way: "The people have taken their faith in the
living God and have reduced it to trust in a building. . . . They believe
that the temple in Jerusalem will keep them safe. They are putting their
trust in the outward trappings of religion."[1]

All this was revealed in the gross immorality of these would-be worshipers. The people were violating God's commandments with vigor,
without a thought as to how it might affect their relationship with God,
simply because they had the temple in their midst. In just two verses of
this sermon, six of the ten commandments are listed as being habitually
broken: "Will you steal, murder, commit adultery, swear falsely, make
offerings to Baal, and go after other gods that you have not known, and
then come and stand before me in this house, which is called by my
name, and say, 'We are delivered!'—only to go on doing all these abom-

inations?" (vv. 9-10). The record of Jeremiah's era shows that it was not safe to do these detestable things—it is never safe for God's people to flout His laws—for God removed even a glorious institution like the temple when it was serving as a cover for godlessness, both in terms of truth and of lifestyle.

This brings a sober message to Christians in every era, but especially to our own age when so many are convinced of God's blessing regardless of our fidelity to His Word. How much of our religious confidence today is invested in institutions rather than in God—in this parachurch organization, in that college or seminary, in our denominations and even in our church buildings, good things that cease to be good when put in God's place. Yet none of our institutions compare to the spiritual glory of the temple of the Lord. God's people vigorously supported the alumni fund of the temple of the Lord. It was the temple they lauded, and on its very presence they trusted; but God was willing to tear the temple down when the people turned their hearts from Him to it. How much more willing is He, then, to take His Spirit from our midst and send our congregations and organizations into the spiritual exile that looms so near?

It was not safe to do these detestable things—it is never safe for God's people to flout His laws—for God removed even a glorious institution like the temple when it was serving as a cover for godlessness, both in terms of truth and of lifestyle.

"GO BACK TO SHILOH"

The prophetic voice was one of warning, God giving His people every opportunity to return in faith, patiently teaching and exhorting them, that they might turn from their ways. Jeremiah's temple sermon includes a classic warning that is especially relevant to us:

> "Go now to my place that was in Shiloh, where I made my name dwell at first, and see what I did to it because of the evil of my people Israel. And now, because you have done all these things, declares the LORD, and when I spoke to you persistently you did not listen, and when I called you, you did not answer, therefore I will do to the house that is called by my name, and in which you trust, and to the place that I gave to you and to

your fathers, as I did to Shiloh. And I will cast you out of my sight, as I cast out all your kinsmen, all the offspring of Ephraim."

—vv. 12-15

Here was a history lesson intended to motivate a change of heart. God pointed back in time to show what He would do when His people turned away, to show how He responds to mere religious observance without spiritual and moral obedience. "Go back to Shiloh," He said in essence, referring to a place where the ark of the covenant—the heart of the temple—had once been set up. Joshua 18:1 tells us, "Then the whole congregation of the people of Israel assembled at Shiloh and set up the tent of meeting there." This is where the high priest Eli served the Lord; here young Samuel was called to God's service.

Why was the temple built in Jerusalem instead of at Shiloh? Why was Shiloh no longer the place of God's presence? Jeremiah's warning explains: "Because of the evil of my people Israel" (v. 12). Because of Eli's faithless leadership, God allowed the holy ark to fall into the hands of the Philistines; as they were always prone to do, the people of Israel thought of it as a magic charm, an artifact that worked regardless of their spiritual and moral condition. God stunned the community at Shiloh by taking away His presence and delivering His people to their enemies. This would happen again in their time, Jeremiah warned, if the people relied merely on the institutions and the machinery of religion rather than turning their hearts to God in true worship and obedience.

Shiloh looms before every faithless generation. Regardless of how impressive religious institutions are, when God abandons them they can be lost in a moment. Once our hearts have turned away from God, once we stop living in holy ways, once we seek not His approval through truth and godliness but rather seek the ABC's of worldly success, we stand in grave jeopardy of losing the things we have so fondly trusted in the place of God—our institutions and endowments and buildings and empires. When these are placed first, when success nudges aside what is faithful to God, then God may write *Shiloh* upon our churches and organizations, having delivered us over to the world we have loved.

In his excellent presentation of Jeremiah's message for today, Philip

G. Ryken reminds us of how many Shilohs we have as well, which ought to remind us of our own danger. He writes:

> There are Shilohs all around the post-Christian West. There are Shilohs, for example, in Oxford, England. Down the Cowley Road there is a large Methodist church where revival meetings used to be held; now it is a full-time bingo parlor. Down the Headington Road there is a Baptist church that has become an Islamic mosque.
>
> There is a Shiloh in Cape May, New Jersey. The Admiral, an immense Christian conference center, used to dominate the Cape May skyline. But the Admiral has been destroyed. The property has been subdivided into housing lots.
>
> There are dozens of Shilohs in Philadelphia. There is a Shiloh at 15th and Locust, where the old First Presbyterian Church used to stand. Now it is a parking garage. . . . There is a Shiloh at 22nd and Walnut, where an Episcopal church has been torn down and replaced by a Sunoco mini-mart. The steeple of the old church is visible only in the mural on the wall next to the store. The church has become a shadow in the city, nothing more than a reflection in a painted window on an urban wall.

Ryken concludes his tour of Shilohs with powerful words that press home the message: "This is an example for the Western church, which has fallen on pagan times. What the church needs now is not building programs or new methods of church growth. What the church needs now is reformation."[2]

Once our hearts have turned away from God, once we stop living in holy ways, once we seek not His approval through truth and godliness but rather the ABC's of worldly success, we stand in grave jeopardy of losing the things we have so fondly trusted in the place of God.

REFORMATION OF WORSHIP AND LIFE

That was Jeremiah's message at the temple: "Amend your ways and your deeds, and I will let you dwell in this place" (7:3). The call to reformation targeted two key areas: the worship and the lives of the people.

The people were worshiping falsely, worshiping God according to the structures and patterns and values of pagan idolatry, just as the church today has sought a marriage of Disney and Freud to bring the people in and keep them happy. It is no wonder, then, that the people were living falsely, mimicking the culture and lifestyle of the pagan peoples around them. They ignored social justice and practiced a moral code that tolerated gross sin: "Will you steal, murder, commit adultery, swear falsely, [and] make offerings to Baal?" the prophet lamented (v. 9). They had forgotten God's commandments, just as the church has done today. Surveys show that an alarming minority of evangelical Christians can recite the Ten Commandments, though they may insist upon having them posted in public buildings. Indeed, some surveys reveal that one is *more* likely to argue for relativism in morals and truth if he has described himself as a born-again Christian. "There are no absolutes" has literally become the motto of the church!

An alarming minority of evangelical Christians can recite the Ten Commandments. "There are no absolutes" has literally become the motto of the church.

"Reform, therefore!" cries the prophet, speaking to our beliefs and our lifestyles, and especially our attitude toward religion and God. If we will not reform, the record of the Bible declares that we will be just another Shiloh that is abandoned by the God who first was abandoned by us.

The prophet Ezekiel, a contemporary of Jeremiah, is the one who most vividly records the shocking scene of God departing from His temple. In Ezekiel 10 he relates the stunning sight of God's chariot rising up within the temple, gathering up His cloud of glory and going away from the city. "Then the glory of the LORD went out from the threshold of the house, and stood over the cherubim," the prophet writes. "And the cherubim lifted up their wings and mounted up from the earth before my eyes as they went out, with the wheels beside them" (vv. 18-19). Nobody noticed as this terrible event transpired, invisible to all eyes save those of the prophet. As in the lament from the days of Shiloh, the word *Ichabod* was spoken over the temple of God in Jerusalem: "The glory has departed from Israel," because the ark and the presence of the Lord were no more (1 Sam. 4:21). This is God's warning, His prophetic call for His church to reform in worship and in life.

THE KING AGAINST THE PROPHET

Deformation takes place despite the sounding voice of the prophet of God. The key issue, therefore, is how the people and especially the leaders respond to that voice and that call to reformation. In Jeremiah's experience we see three ways in which faithless leaders seek to turn aside the people's hearts from the word of warning.

First, we find that false leaders and prophets deceive God's people with *words of false comfort*. We need look no further than the temple sermon we have already considered. Jeremiah 7:4 warned, "Do not trust in these deceptive words: 'This is the temple of the LORD, the temple of the LORD, the temple of the LORD.'" Verse 10 records the comforting assurance, "We are delivered," even while the people immersed themselves in "abominations."

All through Jeremiah's ministry he opposed the vain comfort given by false prophets. He says of them, "They have healed the wound of my people lightly, saying, 'Peace, peace,' when there is no peace" (Jer. 6:14). Jeremiah 28 records his confrontation with the false prophet Hananiah, who prophesied God's intention to destroy the power of the king of Babylon, the enemy Jeremiah had prophesied would come to visit God's judgment on the city. Hananiah gave assurances of divine favor and a complete reversal of the bad fortune they had already experienced—all without addressing the gross spiritual problems of his day. This practice is ever the sign of the false prophet: enticing words that accommodate idolatry among God's people, along with promises of salvation, but without the need for repentance and renewal of faith. In our own time this takes the form of glib assumptions of divine favor—"God bless America"—devoid of repentance for our sin and a true return to the Lord in genuine faith.

Jeremiah fiercely rebuked the false prophet, predicting that within the year he would die for preaching rebellion against the Lord (v. 16). Long before Hananiah's rosy predictions showed any sign of coming true, his false words were revealed by his own predicted death. What a serious thing it is to speak falsely in the name of the Lord!

This practice is ever the sign of the false prophet: enticing words that accommodate idolatry among God's people, promises of salvation, but without the need for repentance and renewal of faith.

The second way the faithless leaders tried to avoid Jeremiah's prophetic call was by simply *rejecting and attacking his message*. This is perhaps best seen in the events of Jeremiah 36, during the reign of Jehoiakim son of Josiah. God had directed the prophet to write his message on a scroll and have it delivered to the people. "It may be," God tenderly reasoned, "that the house of Judah will hear all the disaster that I intend to do to them, so that every one may turn from his evil way, and that I may forgive their iniquity and their sin" (v. 3). This occurred far along the path of deformation, very late in the tale of the people's infidelity. Yet look at how ready God is to forgive their sin and set them back upon a good and blessed way!

Accordingly, Jeremiah set to work along with his faithful servant Baruch. Jeremiah dictated his entire prophetic message—and it is quite a lot of material—and Baruch wrote it all down. Perhaps here are the origins of our written record of Jeremiah's astonishing ministry. Himself unable to be seen in public lest he be imprisoned, the prophet sent his helper to the temple, there to read the words that came from God. "It may be that their plea for mercy will come before the LORD, and that every one will turn from his evil way," he said, "for great is the anger and wrath that the LORD has pronounced against this people" (36:7). We can only imagine the intensity of Jeremiah's prayers, the tears of longing that flowed as he waited for the report of how the people received his scroll.

Baruch faithfully read the message before the people. As news spread, some royal officials asked him to come and read it to them, which he did. The officers, moved by the words and fearful for the prophet's safety, arranged for Baruch and Jeremiah to go into hiding while they took the scroll of the prophet before the king. The scroll therefore made its way into the presence of the king himself, where this terrible scene transpired:

> *Then the king sent Jehudi to get the scroll, and he took it from the chamber of Elishama the secretary. And Jehudi read it to the king and all the officials who stood beside the king. It was the ninth month, and the king was sitting in the winter house, and there was a fire burning in the fire pot before him. As Jehudi read three or four columns, the king would cut them off with a knife and throw them into the fire in the fire pot, until the entire scroll was consumed in the fire that was in the fire pot.*
>
> —36:21-23

What a terrible scene from the highlight film of deformation history. Even this late, God in His grace gave a precious opportunity to repent. But the king would not repent, would not come before the Lord in tears seeking grace. Instead he ordered the arrest of Jeremiah and his servant, but he could not find them since "the LORD hid them" (v. 26). Sadly, that scene is repeated in churches all across our land when an elder or deacon or layperson comes forth and says, "Shouldn't we listen to this message from God's Word?" And yet, citing some scholarly report or church management guide or simply the conventional wisdom of the day, the voice of the prophet is dismissed, even rejected and attacked.

God replied with anger to this king, promising death and destruction to him and his followers. God's anger always burns when His Word is mocked and tossed upon the logs of our vain and worldly pride. Centuries later the apostle Paul condemned men such as this, writing to Timothy: "These men also oppose the truth, men corrupted in mind and disqualified regarding the faith. But they will not get very far, for their folly will be plain to all" (2 Tim. 3:8-9).

Finally, persistence on the part of God's prophet always leads to the third response—namely, *rejecting and attacking the prophet himself.* Having rejected God's message with such flaming indignation, the Jehoiakims of every age are always sure to seek out the messenger with similar intentions. This is precisely what happened to Jeremiah, for the simple reason that he refused to say what the king wanted to hear.

In Jeremiah 37, Zedekiah, the new King of Judah, sent a messenger to Jeremiah to have him pray for Jerusalem and seek God's help against Nebuchadnezzar who, despite the earlier false prophecies, was drawing near to destroy the city. Jeremiah, however, simply reiterated his message that the Lord had given Jerusalem over and that it would be destroyed. Here is Jeremiah's unpopular reply:

> *Thus says the LORD, Do not deceive yourselves, saying, "The Chaldeans will surely go away from us," for they will not go away. For even if you should defeat the whole army of Chaldeans who are fighting against you, and there remained of them only wounded men, every man in his tent, they would rise up and burn this city with fire."*
>
> —JER. 37:9-10

As we might expect, the king's men were appalled at this message, and they responded by arresting Jeremiah for treason. This goes on all the time today, albeit in a different manner. A group of evangelical leaders will, for instance, issue a public statement that betrays the Gospel. Others stand up and oppose what they have done, and what is the cry? "You are traitors! You are not saying nice things to us! You are criticizing us publicly. You are not being winsome, and so you must be shunned and opposed!" They threw Jeremiah into the cistern and left him there to die.

Then the officials said to the king, "Let this man be put to death, for he is weakening the hands of the soldiers who are left in this city, and the hands of all the people, by speaking such words to them. For this man is not seeking the welfare of this people, but their harm."

—38:4

Jeremiah was labeled a traitor because he spoke critically. They said he was not seeking the good of the people—he was not seeking peace. But who, indeed, did not seek the good of the people? Was it not those who refused to hear the Word of the Lord?

A great principle of deformation is that it is more important to be winsome, more excellent to be pleasing in the sight of men, than to guard and proclaim the truth of God.

Few of us are eager to proclaim ourselves prophets, and yet it is the duty of Christians—and especially of ministers in the church—to serve in the office of the prophets, voicing truth from God's Word to the church. Yet there is a great principle of deformation that always opposes this calling, a principle that is especially influential in our own day. This is the idea that it is more important to be winsome, more excellent to be pleasing in the sight of men, regardless of what you do or say, than it is to guard and proclaim the truth of God. Just as in Jeremiah's day, the pragmatists and the lovers of the new and the allies of the world hate and attack the prophetic voice because it unsettles the people. "Your words mark you as a traitor," they said to Jeremiah, and so they still say today.

If there is one certainty in the Evangelical Movement today, it is that those who confront error and compromise, those who deliver bad though biblical news, just like those reformers the prophets, will be cast aside, will be mocked and abused, will be denied access to major media, will be ridiculed and marginalized, just as the prophets of old were put to death with stones and cast into cisterns. Indeed, as Jesus Himself lamented, this treatment of prophets is veritably the spectator sport of deformation history.

A statement like this always requires qualification lest it be mistaken or misrepresented. The true Christian ministry is never mean-spirited or vindictive but rather embraces charity and moderation and long-suffering. A fair reading of Jeremiah will show just these attributes resident in his ministry. But we are also called to guard a trust with our very lives and reputations, "let[ting] goods and kindred go, this mortal life also," as Luther put it in "A Mighty Fortress Is Our God." We do this all for the sake of the Gospel, which alone is the pearl of great price and is thus more than worthy of any such sacrifice.

We are called to guard a trust with our very lives and reputations, "let[ting] goods and kindred go, this mortal life also," all for the sake of the Gospel, which alone is the pearl of great price and is thus more than worthy of any such sacrifice.

It is instructive, I think, that many of the men most useful to God in church history have been somewhat less than winsome in their handling of people. Isaiah spoke blunt truth along with his soaring eloquence; once God had this prophet wander the country naked for three years crying out judgment (see Isa. 20)! What an attractive figure Ezekiel cut while he lay on his side for 390 days straight to symbolize the siege of Jerusalem, cooking his food with manure (see Ezek. 4)! Athanasius, in the ancient church, stubbornly stood against the whole world. *Athanasius contra mundum* is a motto of costly fidelity in an hour of darkness. We, too, may have to embrace another reformation slogan— namely, "One man with God is a majority." Wycliffe, Luther, and Knox were sometimes bizarre and strange figures. They offended and cajoled, they confronted and scolded. I have often reflected on what poor dinner guests these men would make, how horrified most of us would be to have them date our sister. No doubt these flawed men would have done better sometimes to have been more winsome and careful in their words. But they were mightily used of God. They like Paul would have queried,

"Am I now seeking the approval of man, or of God? Or am I trying to please man? If I were still trying to please man, I would not be a servant of Christ" (Gal. 1:10).

It is a good thing to be nice and friendly and mild, but faithfulness to the Gospel is better yet. The commandment "Thou shalt above all be winsome" is a major principle of deformation in every age, just as in the days of Jeremiah, and one that is offended at great risk of harm.

Many confuse an unwillingness to accommodate false leaders with a hard and uncaring spirit. But a study of Jeremiah shows both his willingness to confront deformation and the cost this true prophet paid within his heart. This was the tension that made Jeremiah "the weeping prophet"—both the boldness of his confrontation and the love for his people as he longed for their repentance and salvation with tearful prayers. Geerhardus Vos said of him, "There always seems to have remained in his mind a scar of the tragic conflict between the stern things without and the tender things within. His soul sometimes found it difficult to enter self-forgetfully into the message."[3]

It is certainly true, as Francis Schaeffer emphasized, that we must only confront error and infidelity with a tear in our eye and a humble confession of the beam that is there as well, with care and prayer and consultation with wise fellow believers. Nonetheless, as Jeremiah shows us, expressions of love and unity at the expense of truth are no love at all and no friendship to God.

We must only confront deformation with a tear in our eye and a humble confession of the beam that is there as well. Nonetheless, expressions of love and unity at the expense of truth are no love at all and no friendship to God.

Politically correct winsomeness panders to our pride; it placates the hubris of the self-absorbed. If we are truly humble, we will welcome corrections from the Word of God. As Proverbs says, "Faithful are the wounds of a friend" (27:6). Surely none of us are so excellent in our theology, or at least so pure in our motives, that we should not welcome daily reproof by one speaking from the Bible. The Word of God "discern[s] the thoughts and intentions of the heart" (Heb. 4:12), and surely we should regularly wish to hear this voice—not stoning the prophets or casting them away into cisterns as the king did to Jeremiah, but seating them by our side and close to our ear.

THE PROPHET ABANDONED AND DELIVERED

Jeremiah paid a price, just as everyone will who stands for truth in a relativistic, idolatrous age. He suffered the pain of rejection, the heartache and frustration of a faithful but apparently unsuccessful ministry. He suffered great persecution as well, for the king finally got his hands on God's prophet.

Jeremiah 38 records Jeremiah's terrible imprisonment in an underground cistern filled with mud, while above him the Babylonian invaders were preparing to break through the walls into the city. "So they took Jeremiah and cast him into the cistern of Malchiah, the king's son, which was in the court of the guard, letting Jeremiah down by ropes. And there was no water in the cistern, but only mud, and Jeremiah sank in the mud" (v. 6). What a terrible fate for the man of God, and yet it was by no means exceptional. As Jesus would later point out, such violence marked Jerusalem's common response to the true prophet's voice.

The point of this opposition was to silence once and for all the prophetic voice and its "treason" against the rulers and king. "Let this man be put to death," they argued. "He is weakening the hands of the soldiers who are left in this city, and the hands of all the people, by speaking such words to them. For this man is not seeking the welfare of this people, but their harm" (v. 4). Perhaps afraid to shed the blood of so eminent a man of God, they cast him away to a slow and miserable and hopefully silent death.

We must recognize this as a normal, though terrible, situation for those who stand for God in a godless age, and especially for those who stand in the church against the tide of deformation. "A servant is not greater than his master," Jesus said. "If they persecuted me, they will also persecute you" (John 15:20). Paul spoke of this with great poignancy, writing to his disciple Timothy about what to expect in the age of the church to come. Notice that when he speaks of opponents of the Gospel, he speaks of people within the church:

Indeed, all who desire to live a godly life in Christ Jesus will be persecuted, while evil people and impostors will go on from bad to worse, deceiving and being deceived. But as for you, continue in what you have learned and have firmly believed, knowing from whom you learned it and how from childhood you have been acquainted with the sacred writings, which are able to make you wise for salvation through faith in Christ Jesus. . . . Preach the word; be ready in season and out of season; reprove, rebuke, and exhort, with complete patience and teaching. For the time is coming when people will not endure sound teaching, but having itching ears they will accumulate for themselves teachers to suit their own passions, and will turn away from listening to the truth and wander off into myths. As for you, always be sober-minded, endure suffering, do the work of an evangelist, fulfill your ministry.

—2 TIM. 3:12—4:5

Many think the apostle refers to a special time of difficulty that will come just before the end, but it is better taken to refer generally to the church age. Timothy needed to be prepared for deformation, and the record of God's people—in the Bible and in church history—bears this out.

But even in his cistern Jeremiah was not silenced. By his predicament God was symbolizing the plight of the city. Sinking down into the mud, Jeremiah was abandoned and apparently without hope; surrounded by hostile, powerful enemies and himself wallowing in mire, he poignantly depicted Jerusalem's dire situation.

Jeremiah's experience also depicts God's deliverance for His servants even in the midst of great tragedies in the church. Jeremiah was like Jerusalem in his sad predicament, but whereas God did not rescue Jerusalem, He did deliver Jeremiah. God sent a servant to pull the miserable prophet out of his wretched cell. A man named Ebed-Melech, which appropriately means "Servant of the King," went to the prophet and pulled him out of the cistern. Whereas the city, having forgotten God, was forgotten and abandoned by Him in their trial, God remembered the prophet who remembered and served Him. Surely this is meant to encourage all who stand firm for the Lord, though marginalized and forgotten in the world and even in the church.

In this experience, Jeremiah pointed forward to another prophet who was to come. How like our Lord Jesus on the cross was the prophet in his cistern: surrounded by enemies, parched by thirst, abandoned by both man and, apparently, by God (cf. Ps. 22:12-16). This is the calling of all who would stand with and for Christ in the world. Paul put it in terms of this aspiration: "that I may know him and the power of his resurrection, and may share his sufferings, becoming like him in his death, that by any means possible I may attain the resurrection from the dead" (Phil. 3:10-11). Jeremiah's release from the cistern foreshadows a much greater deliverance, the resurrection of our precious Lord Jesus from the bonds of death. And Christ's resurrection is itself a promise for all who stand for Him and His Word in this world, and sometimes in a church that refuses His voice. Thus all who have fellowship in Christ's death through suffering and abuse may be sure of a share in His glorious resurrection.

In this experience, Jeremiah pointed forward to another prophet who was to come. Jeremiah's release from the cistern foreshadows the resurrection of our precious Lord from the bonds of death. And Christ's resurrection is itself a promise for all who stand for Him and His Word in this world.

"AMEN" AND "AMEN"

Thus ends the history that began with such promise on the fields of Moab, a downward slide into depravity and unbelief, idolatry and apostasy, resulting in the destruction of the very city of God on earth, Jerusalem, along with its magnificent temple. There is no happy ending in this story—though there is in another that would come. The reasons are there for us to see: infidelity to God and idolatry with the world, while God's correcting prophetic voice was opposed, rejected, and attacked. Here we have the precursor to those dreadful, sad words of Jesus, looking out over this very city after it was restored many centuries later: "O Jerusalem, Jerusalem, the city that kills the prophets and stones those who are sent to it! How often would I have gathered your children together as a hen gathers her brood under her wings, and you would not! See, your house is left to you desolate" (Matt. 23:37-38). Jeremiah's own sadness would provide the Old Testament's most poignant lament:

> *How lonely sits the city that was full of people!. . . . Judah has gone into exile because of affliction and hard servitude; she*

dwells now among the nations, but finds no resting place. . . . The
LORD has afflicted her for the multitude of her transgressions.

—LAM. 1:1-5

Perhaps the best way to summarize this sad story is to return to that epic scene when the tribes of Israel assembled on the two hills in Samaria, Mount Ebal and Mount Gerizim. There all the people gathered in accordance with the Word of God through Moses. On Mount Ebal half stood to read the curses for disobedience to God—the curse on those who commit idolatry—and all the people said, "Amen"; the curse for adultery—and the people said, "Amen." On and on went the curses for sin—for faithlessness, for immorality, for dishonest gain. And after each curse upon disobedience, the assembled people cried, "Amen." Then on Mount Gerizim, the other half of the people read the blessings for faithful obedience. Again the people cried, "Amen" (Deut. 27; Josh. 8:30-34).

In the ministry of Jeremiah, God sadly recalled this epochal event. Generations and generations afterward, we read in Jeremiah that God remembered His covenant. What He established in forming His people, He intended for the ages; both the promises and the curses were still written within His mind. "You shall say to them," he told the prophet, "Thus says the LORD, the God of Israel: Cursed be the man who does not hear the words of this covenant that I commanded your fathers when I brought them out of the land of Egypt, from the iron furnace." And how poignant was Jeremiah's reply: "So be it" [or "Amen], LORD" (Jer. 11:3-5).

Just as Israel had witnessed the warnings against sin and rebellion, so the prophet was compelled to give his "Amen" to the guilty verdict and its consequences. The Lord then rendered His commentary on all of this wretched tale: "For I solemnly warned your fathers when I brought them up out of the land of Egypt, warning them persistently, even to this day, saying, Obey my voice. Yet they did not obey or incline their ear, but everyone walked in the stubbornness of his evil heart. Therefore I brought upon them all the words of this covenant, which I commanded them to do, but they did not" (11:7-8).

This is a tale of deformation. It is not mere history, but a warning for the church that strays from faith in God, that turns to the world for its means and for its ends. Paul wrote to Timothy, speaking of two great realities, one of grace and another of corresponding obligation: "God's firm foundation stands, bearing this seal: 'The Lord knows those who are his,' and, 'Let everyone who names the name of the Lord depart from iniquity'" (2 Tim. 2:19). The true, elect church is the flock that knows the Shepherd's voice and follows Him in paths of righteousness.

J. Gordon McConville titled his excellent study of the Deuteronomic theology *Grace in the End*. The title makes the point that for all the harsh reality of blessings and curses, it is not these that come in the end of that history but rather God's grace. He points out that Deuteronomy 27—28, which sets forth the blessings for obedience and the much longer section of curses for disobedience, is followed by a great statement of grace that restores and overcomes the sins of God's people. Deuteronomy 30 especially foretells history to come, promising a return of God's people from exile, no matter how far they are sent from their land. "Then the LORD your God will restore your fortunes and have compassion on you, and he will gather you again from all the peoples where the LORD your God has scattered you" (v. 3). Verse 6 especially foretells a new age to come in which "The LORD your God will circumcise your heart and the heart of your offspring, so that you will love the LORD your God with all your heart and with all your soul, that you may live."

McConville describes this as a "vision of a new hope for Israel on the other side of the failures of its history from settlement to exile."[4] The point, stated so far back in the foundation of His people, is that God has the answer to deformation. He has a solution to the curses of sin that fall so heavily on His people. Here in the shadows of the Old Testament Law is found the encouragement needed for those who have sinned, the hope apart from which none of us can expect to live, the incentive to repent and return for all who have strayed.

There is no happy ending in this story—though there is in another that would come. God has the answer to deformation. He has a solution to the curses of sin that fall so heavily on His people.

Jeremiah in the cistern symbolized the cursed people of God; in his misery the prophet cried "Amen" to God's words of condemnation. But there is another who not only symbolized but actually bore those curses, one who said "Amen" to the work God gave Him, which He faithfully completed on the cursed tree of His cross. Paul writes in Galatians 3:13, "Christ redeemed us from the curse of the law by becoming a curse for us—for it is written, 'Cursed is everyone who is hanged on a tree.'" On the cross of Calvary—to which Jesus Christ was consigned by worldly-minded officials and condemned by a weak, unrighteous ruler on the charge of sedition for preaching God's Word— the Great Prophet and Son of God not only took our curse but gave His "Amen" to the blessing through His own perfect obedience. It is in Him that we may stand firm upon the mount of blessing. Therefore, it is in Him that we may hear the prophetic voice of His Word, calling His church to remember and repent. Jesus is the only answer to the curse of faithless deformation, but His saving work also provides the great motive to return to His ways, that He might be praised in this world. Paul thus concludes, "For all the promises of God find their Yes in him. That is why it is through him that we utter our Amen to God for his glory" (2 Cor. 1:20). Amen.

PART TWO

Reformation in the Old and New Testaments

7

THE MODEL KING

The history of God's people from exodus to exile is sadly downhill. Nonetheless there were many bright lights shining in the dark record. In addition to the well-known figures of Joshua and Samuel and David, the Bible records the lives and careers of numerous great reformers. We have briefly encountered faithful Hezekiah, whose reign is sandwiched between two of the most loathsome figures of biblical history, his father Ahaz and his son King Manasseh. Another great light is Josiah, who came to the throne at age eight after a period of singular depravity. After the Exile, Jerusalem was reestablished under the leadership of Sheshbazzar and Jerubbabel and with the ministry of the great reforming prophets Haggai and Zechariah. Two other great postexilic names are Ezra and Nehemiah, who brought biblical order and obedience to the restored community in God's city.

As great as all those men were, there is no figure after the time of David and before the fall of Jerusalem greater than Jehoshaphat, who reigned over Judah from 873-849 B.C. Jehoshaphat was sixth in the line from David and the son of Asa, a righteous and effective king in his own right. Jehoshaphat is particularly noteworthy for being the contemporary of Ahab, the notoriously evil king of Israel, and also of the prophet Elijah. He was a man fitted for the demands of his time; indeed, Jehoshaphat was the kind of man the church requires in every age, a man of humble faith and sincere godliness. One biography says that his reign was characterized "by the religious spirit that pervaded every act of the king, who sought the favor of the Lord in every detail of his life."[1]

Jehoshaphat did not ascend to the throne in years of crisis. Asa had been a godly king, although his later years were his worst. He had become proud and stubborn like Rehoboam and had turned to political alliances with the king of Aram for aid against the northern kingdom of Israel. In this he foreshadowed the later policy of Ahaz. King Asa became repressive at the end of his life, particularly against the prophets who denounced him for these acts of unbelief.

Jehoshaphat came to the throne at age thirty-five and quickly became a strong and well-established king. What is most impressive about him is that right from the start of his reign he began a program of reformation that would continue throughout his twenty-five years. He was not waiting around for deformation to sink in. Rather, Jehoshaphat knew that unbelief and apostasy had to be attacked at all times, that a king had always to watch, always to be reforming. He knew that hardness of heart and unbelief are not seasonal afflictions that only strike men and nations occasionally. Perhaps he had observed his father's later failings and was therefore wary of sin's power and deceitfulness.

THE PRIORITY OF GOD'S WORD

Jehoshaphat is an ideal model for a reforming leader, for in his reign we find all the elements of biblical reformation. Whereas deformation comes in a great variety of forms and appearances, the Bible shows us a singular model of faithful leadership that fosters reformation among God's people. The most thorough account of his reign is found in 2 Chronicles, beginning in chapter 17, and here we find that Jehoshaphat built his work on the teaching of God's Word.

> *In the third year of his reign he sent his officials, Ben-hail, Obadiah, Zechariah, Nethanel, and Micaiah, to teach in the cities of Judah; and with them the Levites. . . . And they taught in Judah, having the Book of the Law of the LORD with them. They went about through all the cities of Judah and taught among the people.*
> —2 CHRON. 17:7-9

Scholars believe that the third year of Jehoshaphat's reign was the first in which he reigned as sole king, having served as co-regent to his father for the first two. Therefore it seems that this was practically his first policy initiative as new king, marking him as an ideal ruler according to the Deuteronomic model. So long before on the plains of Moab

God decreed in Deuteronomy what a king was to be and to do: "When he sits on the throne of his kingdom, he shall write for himself in a book a copy of this law, approved by the Levitical priests. And it shall be with him, and he shall read in it all the days of his life, that he may learn to fear the LORD his God by keeping all the words of this law and these statutes, and doing them" (Deut. 17:18-19).

Jehoshaphat sent his own officials so that his royal authority was there to commend God's Word. With those officials were priests, who along with their specific religious duties were teachers of the Bible (see Deut. 33:10). "They went about through all the cities of Judah and taught among the people" (2 Chron. 17:9), as the principal means of returning God's people to faithfulness. The "Book of the Law of the LORD" mentioned in 2 Chronicles is surely the book of Deuteronomy itself, which Jehoshaphat had first placed close to his own heart and now set before the hearts of the people.

There is a clear emphasis here not only on the reading of God's Word, but on teaching it and explaining its meaning to the people. In short, Jehoshaphat established a faithful preaching ministry. Where did the king get an idea for this, which seems to have fallen into neglect under his father? Surely he got it from his own study of the Bible. Surely he had considered the fact that he would someday be king and would therefore be responsible for the spiritual health of the nation. Perhaps he consulted with priests he respected and turned to the Law of Moses for instruction. There he would have seen that the foremost qualification of a godly king was his commitment to God's Word. Perhaps as he continued in his preparation for assuming the throne, Jehoshaphat ran across Psalm 19, penned by his great ancestor, King David. There he would have read this wonderful description of God's Word, commending its usefulness for reforming God's people:

> *The law of the Lord is perfect, reviving the soul;*
> *the testimony of the Lord is sure, making wise the simple;*
> *the precepts of the Lord are right, rejoicing the heart;*
> *the commandment of the Lord is pure, enlightening the eyes;*
> *the fear of the Lord is clean, enduring forever;*
> *The rules of the Lord are true and righteous altogether.*
> *More to be desired are they than gold,*
> *even much fine gold;*

sweeter also than honey,
and drippings of the honeycomb.
Moreover, by them is your servant warned;
in keeping them there is great reward.

—*vv. 7-11*

What else could be commended to this superlative degree! What else that can be placed in our hands is described as *perfect, sure, right, pure, clean, true and righteous altogether.* And what else has such power—*reviving the soul, making wise the simple, rejoicing the heart,* and *enlightening the eyes.* Surely these things commended God's Word to Jehoshaphat both for himself and for the edification of his people. It is obvious that he realized this and thus made the teaching of God's Word the first priority of his reign.

What else but the Bible is described as perfect, trustworthy, right, radiant, pure, and sure? And what else has such power— reviving the soul, making wise the simple, giving joy to the heart and light to the eyes, enduring forever in righteousness?

This is where reformation always starts—with the teaching of God's Word so that it is understood and believed by the people. Churches committed to honoring the Lord and serving Him faithfully will always make a strong, biblical, teaching pulpit ministry their first priority. To this end they will allocate time and other resources, realizing that faithful and effective teaching is difficult and spiritually intensive work, and work upon which the spiritual health of the church utterly depends. Such churches will remove burdens that compete with the pastor's time for study and preparation, will pray for God's blessing on the pulpit, and will sit reverently and expectantly before the exposition of the Scriptures in the church.

In our study of deformation we saw that it is when the people forget God—forget His attributes and especially His great saving work of redemption—that unbelief and idolatry set in. How many of our churches today have concluded that preaching alone doesn't work, but only after their preaching has long forgotten God for supposedly more "relevant" topics like how to succeed at work or find happiness in the home. But there is nothing more relevant to God's people than the knowledge of God and His salvation; the teaching of His Word is therefore the start of recovery in the church.

Reformation always starts with the teaching of God's Word so that it is understood and believed by the people. Churches committed to honoring the Lord and serving Him faithfully will always make a strong, biblical, teaching pulpit ministry their first priority.

This is what we consistently find to be the priority of reformers in the Bible. Years later Josiah would recover the Law that had been lost, and immediately he made provision for its faithful reading and exposition. After the return from exile to Jerusalem another ideal reformer, the priest Ezra, very deliberately and formally gathered the people for the teaching of God's Word. The Bible's record of this is particularly revealing and entirely consistent with the reform of Jehoshaphat. First Ezra made himself a man of God's Word: "Ezra had set his heart to study the Law of the LORD, and to do it and to teach his statutes and rules in Israel" (Ezra 7:10). In the book of Nehemiah we learn what Ezra did to restore the people to God:

And all the people gathered as one man into the square before the Water Gate. And they told Ezra the scribe to bring the Book of the Law of Moses that the LORD had commanded Israel. So Ezra the priest brought the Law before the assembly, both men and women and all who could understand what they heard, on the first day of the seventh month. And he read from it facing the square before the Water Gate from early morning until midday, in the presence of the men and the women and those who could understand. And the ears of all the people were attentive to the Book of the Law . . . and as he opened it all the people stood. And Ezra blessed the LORD, the great God, and all the people answered, "Amen, Amen," lifting up their hands. And they bowed their heads and worshiped the LORD with their faces to the ground . . . the Levites, helped the people to understand the Law, while the people remained in their places. They read from the book, from the Law of God, clearly, and they gave the sense, so that the people understood the reading.
—8:1-8

What an excellent description of true and edifying preaching: They made the Bible clear and gave its meaning so the people could understand. That is the kind of teaching ministry that serves as a foundation for lasting reformation. This is the goal a preacher should have in mind for every sermon—not that the people would be regaled by stories or captivated by pulpit wizardry, but that they should be brought to see and understand the Scriptures and have it pressed upon their hearts. The apostle Paul describes his own approach to preaching in similar terms: "We have renounced disgraceful, underhanded ways. We refuse to practice cunning or to tamper with God's word, but by the open statement of the truth we would commend ourselves to everyone's conscience in the sight of God" (2 Cor. 4:2).

We see this same emphasis on Bible teaching all through the New Testament. In Acts 6 the apostles appointed the deacons to deal with temporal matters because, they said, "It is not right that we should give up preaching the word of God to serve tables . . . we will devote ourselves to prayer and to the ministry of the word" (vv. 2, 4). Perhaps the most striking example comes from the ministry of our Lord Jesus Christ. Short of His dying work on the cross, Jesus' first priority was the teaching of God's Word. At the end of His ministry He prayed to the Father, "Sanctify them in the truth; your word is truth" (John 17:17).

So it was in the time of the Protestant Reformation that the great Reformers—Zwingli, Luther, Calvin—were first and foremost preachers and teachers of the Word of God. This must always be the first and most significant ministry in the church. Jehoshaphat realized this and made teaching God's Word the first priority in his reign.

A MAN OF PRAYER AND FAITH

The second thing that must be said about Jehoshaphat is his reliance on God that is manifested in prayer. This is best revealed in one of the great deliverances recorded in the Old Testament, found in 2 Chronicles 20.

A vast army of allied nations from the east had banned together against Judah. Jehoshaphat, we are told, was alarmed at the news. We are reminded of Ahaz in a similar setting, but how different was Jehoshaphat's response to this terrible threat. In an inspiring description we read that "Jehoshaphat. . . . set his face to seek the LORD, and proclaimed a fast throughout all Judah. And Judah assembled to seek help from the LORD; from all the cities of Judah they came to seek the LORD" (vv. 3-4). Jehoshaphat realized that his only help lay with the Lord, and so he summoned a national prayer meeting. We see just how effective his teaching program had been, for the whole people came together to seek help and guidance from God.

Jehoshaphat was faced with a true crisis, but he did not turn to worldly sources of aid, and he did not seek a worldly alliance that would lead to unholy compromises. Rather, he sought the Lord in prayer, together with the people. His prayer—a model for the church—begins in 2 Chronicles 20:6 with an appeal to God's own character: "O LORD, God of our fathers, are you not God in heaven? You rule over all the kingdoms of the nations. In your hand are power and might, so that none is able to withstand you."

Next, in verses 7-9, the king revealed what he had learned about God's saving works in the past, and he brought these before the Lord to ground his appeal: "Did you not, our God, drive out the inhabitants of this land before your people Israel, and give it forever to the descendants of Abraham your friend? And they have lived in it and have built for you in it a sanctuary for your name, saying, 'If disaster comes upon us, the sword, judgment, or pestilence, or famine, we will stand before this house and before you— for your name is in this house—and cry out to you in our affliction, and you will hear and save." What is this but the king praying back to God the very words of Scripture, even the promises found in Deuteronomy of God's help for those who call on Him in faith? Deuteronomy 20:1-4, which the king perhaps recalled in this hour of distress, addresses this very circumstance: "When you go out to war against your enemies, and see horses and chariots and an army larger than your own, you shall not be afraid of them, for the LORD your God is with you, who brought you up out of the land of Egypt . . . 'let not your heart faint. Do not fear or panic or be in dread of them, for the LORD your God is he who goes with you to fight for you against your enemies, to give you the victory.'"

Believing God's Word and taking his stand upon both God's changeless character and His saving works, Jehoshaphat concluded his prayer by pointing out the great coalition gathered against him: "O our God, will you not execute judgment on them? For we are powerless against this great horde that is coming against us. We do not know what to do, but our eyes are on you" (2 Chron. 20:12). What a statement that is—

one we should remember and emulate in our challenges today. Jehoshaphat admitted his weakness and total dependence on the Lord. He did not look upon this crisis as an opportunity to display his own strategic wizardry, but as an opportunity for the Almighty to display His amazing grace. The next verse sums up the occasion with this precious description of a reformed people in utter and faithful reliance on God: "Meanwhile all Judah stood before the Lord, with their little ones, their wives, and their children." Would that it could be said of us today that we stand before the Lord and look for His deliverance.

Jehoshaphat did not look upon this crisis as an opportunity to display his own strategic wizardry, but as an opportunity for the Almighty to display His own amazing grace. "All Judah stood before the Lord, with their little ones, their wives, and their children."

If Jehoshaphat's prayer is a classic of reformation devotion, God's response is equally classic in showing His faithfulness to His believing children:

> *And he [God] said, "Listen, all Judah and inhabitants of Jerusalem and King Jehoshaphat: Thus says the LORD to you, 'Do not be afraid and do not be dismayed at this great horde, for the battle is not yours but God's. Tomorrow go down against them. . . . You will not need to fight in this battle. Stand firm, hold your position, and see the salvation of the LORD on your behalf, O Judah and Jerusalem.' Do not be afraid and do not be dismayed. Tomorrow go out against them, and the LORD will be with you."*
>
> —vv. 15-17

If salvation by grace alone is a great principle ensuring that God is able and willing to save, its corollary on our part is humble and reliant prayer. Here, then, is a vital principle of reformation: a humble reliance on God's power in every trial and danger. This is always manifested in prayer. Therefore a reforming church is a praying church. Jehoshaphat was much in prayer because he really trusted God and not in man-made methods or unholy alliances.

Jehoshaphat did see God's deliverance, and the whole of Judah with him. Second Chronicles 20:21 tells us they went forward the next morning singing, "Give thanks to the LORD, for his steadfast love endures forever." Even as they sang, the Lord "set an ambush" (v. 22) against their enemies, causing them to fight among each other in confusion and driving them into flight. The conclusion to the account is told in these words:

> *When Judah came to the watchtower of the wilderness, they looked toward the horde, and behold, there were dead bodies lying on the ground; none had escaped. When Jehoshaphat and his people came to take their spoil . . . They were three days in taking the spoil, it was so much. . . . Then they returned, every man of Judah and Jerusalem, and Jehoshaphat at their head, returning to Jerusalem with joy, for the LORD had made them rejoice over their enemies. . . . And the fear of God came on all the kingdoms of the countries when they heard that the LORD had fought against the enemies of Israel. So the realm of Jehoshaphat was quiet, for his God gave him rest all around.*
>
> —vv. 24-30

What a great testimony to what a single reforming king could do for Judah, and an encouragement for lonely reformers in the church today. If we would know such victories, enjoy such peace, and exert this kind of witness in our day, surely we must turn to the Lord in times of trouble with the prayerful faith of Jehoshaphat. We, like him, should be able to say from experience the words David penned in Psalm 34:

> *I sought the Lord, and he answered me*
>   *and delivered me from all my fears. . . .*
> *This poor man cried, and the Lord heard him*
>   *and saved him out of all his troubles.*
> *The angel of the Lord encamps*
>   *around those who fear him, and delivers them.*
> *Oh, taste and see that the Lord is good!*
> *Blessed is the man who takes refuge in him!*
> *Oh, fear the Lord, you his saints,*
>   *for those who fear him have no lack.*
>
> —vv. 4-9

A reforming church is always a praying church. Jehoshaphat was much in prayer because he really trusted God and not in man-made methods or unholy alliances.

REFORM OF WORSHIP

In the record of the various kings in the books of Kings and Chronicles, one yardstick is consistently used to evaluate the faithfulness of any given monarch. That yardstick is the king's attitude toward the false worship that had so deeply taken root among the people. Asa, Jehoshaphat's father, distinguished himself for his vigor in cutting down the Asherah poles and ridding the land of the high places where idolatrous rites took place. Ahaz, among the unfaithful kings, was condemned for his descent into pagan practices: "And he did not do what was right in the eyes of the LORD his God, as his father David had done, but he walked in the way of the kings of Israel. He even burned his son as an offering, according to the despicable practices of the nations whom the LORD drove out before the people of Israel. And he sacrificed and made offerings on the high places and on the hills and under every green tree" (2 Kings 16:2-4).

It is essential to realize that people like Ahaz did not cease to worship the Lord. Rather, they sought to pick and choose from the buffet of religious offerings, melding together their own personal plate of spiritual mixtures. People like Ahaz assume there is something to be said for every religion, and that they are better off covering all the bases than taking a decisive stand for any particular one.

Peter Jones writes of a scene that shows how in step our time is with the attitude of men like King Ahaz. At a meeting of the Parliament of the World's Religions, he saw this: "A liberal Presbyterian professor in his long black robe; a Buddhist priest in his orange one; a Catholic cardinal in his royal purple splendor; the high priestess of the goddess Isis in her white robe and pointed headdress—all stood together in celebration of their spiritual unity [while they] held hands and danced around the room to the sound of a Native American Indian shaman's drum."[2] How at home the idolaters of Israel would be in the ecumenical spirit that chants today, "All gods are one; all religions are one; all spirituality leads to the one god."

Jehoshaphat could not have rejected such an attitude more decisively. Like his father, he is singled out for his reform of worship in the life of the people. This flowed from his own personal spiritual integrity, as described in 2 Chronicles 17:3-6: "He did not seek the Baals, but sought the God of his father and walked in his commandments, and not according to the practices of Israel. . . . His heart was courageous in the ways of the LORD. And furthermore, he took the high places and the Asherim out of Judah."

Few people today consider worship a significant target for reform. We are used to worship that mimics our fast-food way of life and says, "Have it your way!" And yet to follow the inclination of our hearts is to flirt with disaster. That was the lesson learned by Nadab and Abihu, the high priest Aaron's sons, when they came before the Lord in the tabernacle with "unauthorized fire" and were struck down by God (Num. 3:4). This is why God gave such precise instructions for worship to Moses and the people, to instruct them in right worship and to protect them from their own foolish and sinful hearts. John Calvin was surely right when he said, "The true rule of religion, as to the worship of God, is, that nothing human is to be mingled, that no one is to bring forward what is his own, or what seems good to himself." The reason for this is that it is God and not man who determines how God is to be worshiped. God's people, knowing their folly and sin, should ever be wary of innovation in worship, "because whatever men devise of themselves is a pollution of divine worship."[3]

Many Christians object to such a restrictive view of worship, arguing that in the New Testament Jesus has demanded simply that worship be done "in spirit and truth" (John 4:24). But worship in truth must surely be worship according to Scripture. Jesus' words, while allowing for a freedom not experienced in the Old Testament, nonetheless give the constraint that our worship must be spiritual and true. His injunction against false worship warns us against two grave dangers seen in the Old Testament—namely, that of worshiping a false god and that of worshiping the true God falsely.

This is a message an increasingly small minority of people will tolerate in our relativistic, utilitarian age. *The Cambridge Declaration*, issued by the Alliance of Confessing Evangelicals, articulates the need for reform of worship in our time, expressed in language Jehoshaphat would surely have understood:

The loss of God's centrality in the life of today's church is common and lamentable. It is this loss that allows us to transform worship into entertainment, gospel preaching into marketing, believing into technique, being good into feeling good about ourselves, and faithfulness into being successful. . . . We must focus on God in our worship, rather than the satisfaction of our personal needs. God is sovereign in worship; we are not. Our concern must be for God's kingdom, not our own empires, popularity or success.[4]

All through Scripture we are warned against man-made forms of worship. In forbidding idolatry, the second commandment (Exod. 20:4-6) "also implicitly forbids all human invention in worship."[5] This, we saw, was the great sin of Jeroboam, employing a system of worship "devised from his own heart" (1 Kings 12:33). In the New Testament, the apostle Paul similarly denounces worship that is "according to human precepts and teachings," with their "appearance of wisdom" and their "self-made religion" (Col. 2:22-23).

Not every novel approach to worship is idolatry, nor is true worship a matter of merely maintaining traditions. The real point is this: Worship is about God and for God's benefit first and foremost. Therefore worship must be intended for His pleasure and according to His Word. It is certainly true that human beings benefit from worship. But if we are going to talk about consumer-driven worship, we must realize that the primary consumer of worship, so to speak, is God Himself. Jehoshaphat understood this and was therefore God-centered in his worship, reforming the worship of his people according to the teaching of God's Word, with biblical means that were aimed toward biblical ends. Any true reform today must include this same emphasis on the reform of worship.

Worship is about God and must be intended for His pleasure and according to His Word. The primary consumer of worship, so to speak, is God Himself. Any true reform today must include this same emphasis on the reform of worship.

ESTABLISHMENT OF JUSTICE AND MERCY

Finally, Jehoshaphat diligently attended to matters of justice and mercy. It is easy for us to forget this, but real reformation always includes such an emphasis. Indeed, notice how closely aligned are a return to God in true faith and worship and an emphasis on social righteousness:

> *Jehoshaphat lived at Jerusalem. And he went out again among the people, from Beersheba to the hill country of Ephraim, and brought them back to the* LORD, *the God of their fathers. He appointed judges in the land in all the fortified cities of Judah, city by city, and said to the judges, "Consider what you do, for you judge not for man but for the* LORD. *He is with you in giving judgment. Now then, let the fear of the* LORD *be upon you. Be careful what you do, for there is no injustice with the* LORD *our God, or partiality or taking bribes."*
>
> —2 CHRON. 19:4-7

This concern for social welfare and justice has historically been a hallmark of real Christian reformation. The sixteenth-century Protestant Reformation promoted political and social justice in every country in which it took root, with an accompanying elevation in general standards of living. It was in order to give common people access to the Bible that literacy grew in nations such as Germany and Scotland. The example of John Calvin's Geneva is especially striking. The city fathers had formally joined the Reformation, but riots and gambling, drunkenness and indecency were still rife in this notoriously dissolute city. Into this setting Calvin came with the Word of God. James Montgomery Boice writes of the powerful work of reform that thoroughly changed the city: "Calvin preached from the Bible every day, and under the power of that preaching the city began to be transformed. As the people of Geneva acquired knowledge of God's Word and were changed by it, the city became, as John Knox called it later, a New Jerusalem from which the gospel spread to the rest of Europe, England, and the New World."[6]

Social reformation is a natural by-product of spiritual reformation, but it is also the result of a deliberate program apart from which the reforming work of the church is incomplete. Calvin, for instance, urged the ruling body of Geneva to regulate sanitary conditions and build a hospital, to introduce industries to provide jobs, and to erect schools to offer education. Jehoshaphat, with his greater powers as king, established a widespread and effective system of justice and mercy that blessed the people while it honored God.

> *Social reformation is a natural by-product of spiritual refor-*
> *mation, but it is also the result of a deliberate program apart*
> *from which the reforming work of the church is incomplete.*

A FLAWED LEGACY OF A GREAT REFORMER

Such was the legacy of a great and godly king. Jehoshaphat made haste in reforming the nation; he prioritized the systematic teaching of God's Word; he relied on the power of the Lord as reflected in his prayer; he faithfully reformed worship and removed the idols; and finally he diligently sought mercy and justice in corporate life. Here is a straightforward biblical agenda for reformation in the church, one that is validated all through the Bible. If we are to be reformers, we must apply ourselves to these very things. "Deal courageously," Jehoshaphat exhorted his officials, "and may the LORD be with the upright" (2 Chron. 19:11).

The best of men, however, are men at best, Jehoshaphat included. However godly and great, he was not a perfect king or reformer. It is mainly in two areas that we see his failures. First, Jehoshaphat engaged in a wrongheaded, sentimental ecumenism that brought him the Lord's displeasure. Second, he failed to provide a faithful leader for the generation that followed. The two failures are related, for it was as a result of his foolish alliance with his godless cousins to the north that Jehoshaphat placed the nation's future in the hands of unbelievers.

Jehoshaphat lived during the reign of Ahab, the wicked king of Israel, husband to Jezebel, nemesis of the great prophet Elijah. Undoubtedly Jehoshaphat was grieved by affairs among the ten northern tribes and the bitter hostility between the two halves of God's people, Israel and Judah. Jehoshaphat was like so many people today who are dismayed by our divisions and denominations, and he tried to heal the breach as he was able. Unfortunately, he failed to realize that the cause of this disunion was deeper than what could be healed with a little diplomacy.

> *"The unity that our Lord is concerned about is a unity which*
> *is spiritual. . . . It is a unity of people who . . . first of all are*
> *united to Christ and made one with him, and, through him, one*
> *with God."*

Many people point out that our Lord Jesus, on the night of His arrest, prayed for unity in the church. "I . . . ask. . . . that they may all be one, just as you, Father, are in me, and I in you" (John 17:20-21). Undoubtedly Jehoshaphat made his journey to Ahab's court in just this spirit; yet his experience warns us to be wise in what kind of unity we labor to bring about. James Boice advises, "True Christians should be united, and it is sad that we are as divided as we are. But when anyone speaks about unity we must be careful to determine what kind of unity we are talking about." Is it a unity in name, in organization, in resources? Boice points to the Middle Ages as an example of how the church's times of greatest outward unity have been among its worst and least faithful days. He concludes, "The only unity that is worth having—the only true unity—is the unity built on the revealed truth of God centering in the person and work of Jesus Christ."[7] Martyn Lloyd-Jones similarly warns:

> A mere coalition of organisations or denominations has in reality nothing whatsoever to do with this unity. Indeed, it may even be a danger. The unity that our Lord is concerned about is a unity which is spiritual. It consists of a unity of spirits, and it is a unity, therefore, which is based solidly upon the truth. . . . It is a unity of people who have become spiritual and who have been born again: we are made one with one another, because we first of all are united to Christ and made one with him, and, through him, one with God.[8]

What a help such advice would have been to Jehoshaphat, for in pursuit of false unity he committed a major and nearly fatal blunder. Second Chronicles 18 begins with this ominous statement: "Now Jehoshaphat had great riches and honor, and he made a marriage alliance with Ahab." Allied with this scheming and unbelieving northern king, Jehoshaphat was soon drawn into a war started on Ahab's initiative. Realizing something of the folly of what he was getting into, Jehoshaphat asked Ahab to seek the counsel of the Lord. Ahab responded by bringing forth no less than four hundred prophets, all of whom heartily agreed with their king's plan, promising, "God will give it [victory] into the hand of the king" (v. 5). Recognizing false prophets when he saw them, Jehoshaphat responded with apparent embarrassment. "Is there not here another prophet of the LORD of whom we may inquire?" he asked. There was one, Ahab admitted, "but I hate him, for he never prophesies good concerning me, but always evil" (vv. 6-7). The true prophet, when summoned, spoke of God's judgment of wicked Ahab and his army: "If you return in peace, the LORD has not spoken by me" (v. 27).

Jehoshaphat went to battle with Ahab and suffered defeat, and Ahab himself died of wounds. When the godly king returned to Jerusalem, God sent a messenger to reprove him for his folly: "Jehu the son of Hanani the seer went out to meet him and said to King Jehoshaphat, 'Should you help the wicked and love those who hate the LORD? Because of this, wrath has gone out against you from the LORD'" (2 Chron. 19:2).

Jehoshaphat's example shows that a false ecumenism—that which preaches unity among those who are not united by true faith and worship—is infidelity to God, however sentimental its motivation. Undoubtedly he justified his actions on the grounds of his desire to influence the unbelieving king of the neighboring kingdom. But his example shows that the bridge of influence always has two lanes. It was Jehoshaphat who was influenced by Ahab; it was Judah's king who was dragged into a foolish war along with his godless ally. Jehoshaphat did not restore the true faith to Israel by his compromising alliance; rather, idolatry took its place on the throne once occupied by the great reformer king. His example shows us that the idea of influence through foolish and ungodly alliances is really a terrible step in the direction of apostasy. As Robert Godfrey has argued in an article titled "The Myth of Influence," "The most tragic consequence of the myth of influence is that those who embrace it often end up being influenced by the world rather than being a good influence on the world."[9] However noble its purported goals, compromise with unbelief or deformation in the church brings not God's blessing on the spiritually naïve, but His wrath on those who seek peace with men instead of fidelity to God.

False ecumenism—that which preaches unity among those who are not united by true faith and worship—is infidelity to the Lord, however sentimental its motivation. "Those who embrace it often end up being influenced by the world rather than being a good influence on the world."

The second of Jehoshaphat's great mistakes was the result of his naïve and unfaithful alliance. As a result of his marriage to a woman from Ahab's house, he provided a successor to his throne, his son King Jehoram, who married one of Ahab's daughters and largely undid all that Jehoshaphat had achieved with such hard labor. What a terrible transition is recorded in 2 Chronicles 21: "Jehoshaphat slept with his fathers and was buried with his fathers in the city of David, and Jehoram his son reigned in his place. . . . And he walked in the way of the kings of Israel, as the house of Ahab had done, for the daughter of Ahab was his wife. And he did what was evil in the sight of the LORD" (vv. 1, 6).

What are we to expect? While Jehoshaphat was busying himself with the affairs of state, fighting wars and otherwise ruling the nation, who was raising his son and heir but his wife (the boy's mother), a woman steeped in the ways of Ahab and Jezebel. Small wonder, then, that after Jehoshaphat died, all his achievements went by the wayside. Within a few years of the great king's death, his halls were trod by the feet of Ahab's advisers, false prophets like those he had encountered in the wicked king's presence, and by a son from his own body who bowed before the idols and led the people away from God.

Jehoshaphat was a great and model reforming king. His reign was a bright light burning amidst a great darkness. But good and faithful as he was, he was not wise in this one grave matter. Thinking to influence and reach wicked Ahab by foolish and ultimately unfaithful means, Jehoshaphat handed over his family, his court, and ultimately the fruit of all his labor into the hands of those who were rebels against the Lord. It is a sober warning to us all that reformation requires both singular devotion to God through His Word and the costly holiness that requires us to be different not only from the world but also from worldly people claiming to serve the cause of Christ. Unless we are willing to stand alone with God if need be, we risk betraying the Lord and sacrificing the legacy of true religion for our children's generation.

8

A FEW GOOD MEN

In the year 640 B.C. an eight-year-old boy named Josiah ascended the throne of Judah. This royal child faced the most difficult of circumstances; the fact that his father had been assassinated by court officials testifies to the chaos surrounding his elevation. However great his distant ancestry in the house of David, Josiah's nearer relations were among the most depraved in all the Bible. His grandfather was Manasseh, perhaps the single most wicked king in the history of the southern kingdom. This ruler was the heir born late in life to godly King Hezekiah, and apparently he profited little from his father's spirituality. Manasseh instituted the most horrific forms of idolatry in Jerusalem, erecting altars to Baal and setting up an Asherah pole in the temple. According to tradition, it was this evil king who hunted and killed the great prophet Isaiah, who had served as a mentor to his father.

The Bible says of Manasseh, "He burned his son as an offering and used fortune-telling and omens and dealt with mediums and with wizards. . . . Manasseh led them astray to do more evil than the nations had done whom the LORD destroyed before the people of Israel. . . . Moreover, Manasseh shed very much innocent blood, till he had filled Jerusalem from one end to another" (2 Kings 21:6, 9, 16). His son Amon was fortunate to escape human sacrifice to the pagan god Molech, into whose fiery hands babies were offered outside the walls of Jerusalem. And yet the Bible says of Amon, "He walked in all the way in which his father walked and served the idols that his father served and worshiped them. He abandoned the LORD, the God of his fathers, and did not walk in the way of the LORD" (2 Kings 21:21-22).

AFTER DARKNESS, LIGHT

Into this situation young Josiah entered as Judah's new king. The Bible says that Jerusalem at this time was actually worse than were the cities of Canaan before the entry of the Israelites—worse than cities like Sodom and Gomorrah, if that is imaginable. No matter how desperate our assessment may be of the church today, our challenges pale before the debauched and apostate condition of Jerusalem at that time. How horrid the situation must have appeared in the eyes of the few godly people, how hopeless the chances of reform from an eight-year-old king arising from such a lineage. Yet, from the longer view of the Bible, it was an ideal setting for God's sovereign grace to be displayed. In this darkest of dark times, God shined the light of His saving mercy into the life of His people, so that now we look back on Josiah as the last and among the greatest of all the reforming kings.

We begin our study of Josiah's career with some questions. Something must account for the faith that blossoms right from the start of his record. Perhaps it was the example and instruction of a godly mother. The only thing we know about Josiah's mother is her name, Jedidah, daughter of Adaiah. We know nothing of her or her family from Scripture, but we would not be surprised to learn that here was a spring of living water. The only hint of godliness in the house of his father Amon comes in the form of the similarity of names between Amon's mother, Meshullemeth, and a man named Meshullam, the grandfather of one of Josiah's most godly officials. Perhaps this speaks of a link to a believing family, difficult as it is to imagine of a wife of Manasseh; and perhaps this woman had just enough influence to arrange her son's marriage to another believing young woman.

We remember as well that, though it is hard to believe, Manasseh repented of his great sins near the end of his life, removed the idols from the temple, and died in the faith (see 2 Chron. 33:10-17). Manasseh is perhaps the Bible's greatest testimony that anyone can repent and believe; as long as there is life, there is yet hope of salvation. Unable to convert his son from the path of his earlier wicked ways, perhaps Manasseh directed his labors to his grandson Josiah, who would have been six years old when Manasseh died. In such a case, the great reforms of Josiah may have been born in the improbable repentance of Judah's most wicked king, who was not beyond the reach of God's saving mercy. As he later did with Saul of Tarsus, perhaps God in His unsearchable wisdom brought glory to Himself by making the chief of sinners a messenger of His grace. This would not be the only time that God's work of repentance and faith in the heart of a single man or woman sent forth ripples that foretold the broader coming of God's kingdom. It reminds us anew that reformation begins in the hearts of individual people, and that no witness, no prayer, no conversion ever takes place without real and vital significance to God's redeeming plan as it works onward in history.

Despite our ignorance of the details, some wonderful working of God's grace must account for the rise of a young and godly ruler in the midst of such chaos. Surely this confirms what the Lord taught Paul in his distress: "My grace is sufficient for you, for my power is made perfect in weakness" (2 Cor. 12:9). However Josiah's conversion came about, we see in him the pattern that is always revealed in times of reformation. The great motto of the sixteenth-century Protestant Reformation expresses it: *post tenebras lux*; that is, *after darkness, light.*

The great reforms of Josiah may have been born in the improbable repentance of Judah's most wicked king, Manasseh, God making the chief of sinners a messenger of His grace. This confirms what the Lord taught Paul: "My grace is sufficient for you, for my power is made perfect in weakness" (2 Cor. 12:9).

It is also not unlikely that seeds of reform may have come from the court officials, who probably came into office during Manasseh's later and godly regime. We are not told why or how Amon was assassinated, but it may have been faithful men who despaired of a return to a situation like that of Manasseh's former reign; perhaps they could think of nothing more to do than slay the father so as to try anew with the son. As we will see, the officials who aided Josiah were followers and supporters of the true prophets, men of faith and resolve in support of the Lord. It is sad to think of godly men resorting to murder, and yet it is quite possible that such people were behind this desperate measure that brought young Josiah to the throne.

These officials must inevitably have overseen Josiah's upbringing and his early years of rule. By his middle twenties it seems the king had come into his own. This is what we find beginning in the eighteenth year of his reign, when the Bible begins recording his royal initiatives. Josiah's very first act, as told by 2 Kings, had to do with the restoration of God's temple, a sure sign of his devotion to the Lord. "In the eighteenth year of King Josiah, the king sent Shaphan the son of Azaliah, son of Meshullam, the secretary, to the house of the LORD, saying, 'Go up to Hilkiah the high priest, that he may count the money that has been brought into the house of the LORD, which the keepers of the threshold have collected from the people . . . and let them give it to the workmen who are at the house of the LORD, repairing the house'" (22:3-5). A remarkable providence was about to take place, one that would define an entire generation, and we are not surprised that it happens in the context of a concern for God's glory. Hilkiah the high priest received this instruction from the king and began the work of restoring the temple. Soon word came from the priest that startled the royal court. "Hilkiah the high priest said to Shaphan the secretary, 'I have found the Book of the Law in the house of the LORD'" (v. 8).

THE RETURN OF THE WORD

Perhaps we see here why Manasseh's efforts at reform had accomplished so little. It is true that this paragon of evil genuinely repented of his sin, a remarkable example that proves it is never too late for anyone to turn to God. Manasseh then tore down the high places and removed the idols from the temple. But it is not enough to merely oppose the darkness; one must also shine the light of God's Word, and this had been lost.

The account of Josiah's reign makes clear that the Scriptures had literally been lost. First came neglect, so that none knew the Word, and probably little care was taken to preserve it and make new copies. Finally the Scriptures disappeared altogether, and no one could even remember where they might be.

The high priest Hilkiah, having providentially stumbled across a scroll of the Law, hastened to see Shaphan, the king's secretary, declaring his find and sending the scroll to the king. It seems that what Hilkiah found was no less than the book of Deuteronomy, the formative charter that established the nation of Israel as God's covenant people. This scroll is simply identified as "the Book of the Law"; yet Josiah's subsequent reform agenda makes it clear that this was indeed Deuteronomy. So clear is the identification that liberal scholars today are nearly unanimous in declaring that Deuteronomy must have been written by Josiah and his advisers, who then made up the story about finding the scroll. This is, of course, mere scholarly invention erected on a foundation of unbelief. From the Bible's perspective, God was providing His servants the very thing they most needed—His own Word for the reformation of His people.

Imagine the scene when the lost Word of God was presented to the young king and man of faith. Josiah, we must presume, had never seen a scroll of the Scriptures, had never heard God's Word read. With what trembling hands must his secretary have unwrapped the material, setting his eyes for the first time on God's holy writ. We can imagine how Josiah might have looked on this as a sign of God's special favor; he was the appointed servant to whom God's own revelation was now restored. But the king responded not with celebration or lofty pride, but with the bitter repentance of a leader who realizes how great has been the offense of his people. The biblical account is sparse and direct:

> *Then Shaphan the secretary told the king, "Hilkiah the priest has given me a book." And Shaphan read it before the king. When the king heard the words of the Book of the Law, he tore his clothes. And the king commanded . . . "Go, inquire of the LORD for me, and for the people, and for all Judah, concerning the words of this book that has been found. For great is the wrath of the LORD that is kindled against us, because our fathers have not obeyed the words of this book, to do according to all that is written concerning us."*
>
> —2 KINGS 22:10-13

Josiah here reveals the heart of a true reformer. He was not merely seeking better days ahead for his people—his heart was pierced by the offense against God when His people departed from His ways. Undoubtedly Josiah was afraid for his people as he heard the words read from the book of Deuteronomy. How great was their sin, and how severe were the curses spoken against the breakers of God's covenant! But greater still was Josiah's mortification at his personal offense against the true and living God. His goal in reform, therefore, was not merely to lead the people into a better way, but more importantly to give God the honor and obedience to which He is due. Like Josiah, true reformers today are motivated primarily by *theology* and *doxology* and only afterward by more practical concerns.

Josiah's officials found a prophetess in Jerusalem, and through her they inquired of the Lord. The reply they received must have chilled their bones, for she informed them that the covenant had indeed been broken, and that the curses it contained would be visited on Judah. Nonetheless God had a message of grace for the king:

> *"'But to the king of Judah, who sent you to inquire of the LORD, thus shall you say to him, Thus says the LORD, the God of Israel: Regarding the words that you have heard, because your heart was penitent, and you humbled yourself before the LORD, when you heard how I spoke against this place and against its inhabitants . . . and you have torn your clothes and wept before me, I also have heard you, declares the LORD. Therefore, behold, I will gather you to your fathers, and you shall be gathered to your grave in peace, and your eyes shall not see all the disaster that I will bring upon this place.'" And they brought back word to the king.*

> —VV. 18-20

A true reformer, Josiah's heart was pierced by the offense against God. Like him, true reformers today are motivated primarily by theology and doxology and only afterward by more practical concerns.

JOSIAH'S REFORMATION

Josiah did not waste time, nor did he take his ease in God's promise to him. Immediately he began the work of reformation, according to the pattern we have already seen in the Bible. The next chapter of 2 Kings begins with a renewal of the covenant, to which Josiah summoned all the elders of Judah and Jerusalem for prayer and the renewing of devotion to the Lord. There at the temple, where Jehoshaphat and all the people had set their eyes upon the Lord in hope, Josiah stood "with . . . all the men of Judah and all the inhabitants of Jerusalem and the priests and the prophets, all the people, both small and great. And he read in their hearing all the words of the Book of the Covenant that had been found in the house of the LORD. And the king stood by the pillar and made a covenant before the LORD, to walk after the LORD and to keep his commandments and his testimonies and his statutes with all his heart and all his soul, to perform the words of this covenant that were written in this book. And all the people joined in the covenant" (23:2-3).

Here again we see the centrality of God's Word in the work of reformation. So vital is the Bible to any true reform that a return to the Bible—to its reverence and study, to its acceptance as the authoritative and sufficient guide for all of our faith and practice, to its use as the yardstick by which all other claims to truth and wisdom are assessed— is precisely what reformation is all about.

A return to the Bible—to its reverence and its study, to its acceptance as the guide for all of our faith and practice, to its use as the yardstick by which all other truths and claims to wisdom are assessed—is precisely what reformation is all about.

Josiah based his whole reforming work on the Word of God and on prayer. It is no surprise, as well, that he urgently attended to the vital matter of the reform of worship. There in the presence of the people, Josiah watched as the priests removed all the articles of idolatrous worship, cleansing God's house and removing the pagan priests. Included was social and moral reform that is always part of the reestablishment of true religion. "And he broke down the houses of the male cult prostitutes who were in the house of the LORD, where the women wove hangings for the Asherah" (v. 7). So thorough was Josiah's purge of false religion that he ground up the Asherah poles and Baal altars, scattering their dust on pagan graves, and went throughout the land systematically destroying the machinery of idolatry on the high places and in the valleys. Second Kings 23 lists item after discarded item, place after place where Josiah went to purge false worship, setting an example for us about the great significance of this aspect of true reformation.

Finally the king arrived at Bethel, appearing before the altars erected three centuries earlier by Jeroboam. There he fulfilled the prophecy given by a man of God from Judah, who long before had prophesied, "Behold, a son shall be born to the house of David, Josiah by name, and he shall sacrifice on you the priests of the high places who make offerings on you, and human bones shall be burned on you" (1 Kings 13:2). That now was fulfilled to the letter, Josiah exhuming the bodies of the pagan priests and burning their bones to defile the altar. Coming upon the tomb of the man of God from Judah, he ordered it alone to be respected, demonstrating God's acceptance of that long-past prophet.

The reform of worship is never a mere matter of removing false practices but is only made complete with the joyful, earnest institution of worship that conforms to the Bible. Josiah did what reformers today must do. Instead of gazing around at the practices of the world for popular modes of praise, he turned his gaze to God's Word. He read it and derived conclusions from it about what ought to be done. Then, as now, the issue was not about style or preference, but about a desire to see God obeyed in the life of His people, and especially as they gathered before Him for worship.

Instead of gazing around at the practices of the world for effective modes of worship, Josiah turned his gaze to the Bible. The issue was not about style or preference, but about a desire to see God obeyed in the life of His people, and especially in worship.

In Josiah's case, this meant the reinstitution of the Old Testament feasts, beginning with the Passover. For us it means the reinstatement of the faithful preaching of God's Word, of Scripture reading and prayer, and of the right administration of the sacraments. The significance of Josiah's reforms are indicated by this statement in the Bible:

> *And the king commanded all the people, "Keep the Passover to the LORD your God, as it is written in this Book of the Covenant." For no such Passover had been kept since the days of the judges who judged Israel, or during all the days of the kings of Israel or of the kings of Judah. But in the eighteenth year of King Josiah this Passover was kept to the LORD in Jerusalem.*
>
> —2 KINGS 23:21-23

Josiah turned back the clock on worship, realizing that what mattered was not keeping up with the times, not incorporating the latest innovations of the idol-praising world, but true worship as revealed by

God in the Bible. What Josiah did, we must do today. We must establish our worship not on contemporary trends and worldly appeal but on the changeless principles, commands, and prohibitions that are given by God Himself, to whom alone our worship is to be offered.

> *For Josiah, reform of worship meant the reinstitution of the Old Testament feasts, beginning with the Passover. For us it means the reinstatement of the faithful preaching of God's Word, of Scripture reading and prayer, and of the right administration of the sacraments.*

Josiah would reign for thirty-one years. Undoubtedly he launched construction projects, engaged in diplomacy, and undertook military action. But it is for this that the Bible remembers him—his reform of God's people on the basis of God's Word, which is commended to future generations. There can be little doubt that Josiah received opposition to these extensive reforms. Some would have thought he was too focused on the details of obedience. Many no doubt complained about abandoning up-to-date practices for the rituals and procedures directed by God's Word, an approach to worship that was strange and unfamiliar to the people. Surely Josiah was accused of worshiping the Bible and of having a spirituality that was too bound up with matters of truth instead of feelings. But there is one assessment of this king that we know for sure because it is recorded forever in the Bible. Here is what God thought of the great reformer-king Josiah:

> *[Josiah] establish[ed] the words of the law that were written in the book that Hilkiah the priest found in the house of the LORD. Before him there was no king like him, who turned to the LORD with all his heart and with all his soul and with all his might, according to all the Law of Moses, nor did any like him arise after him.*
>
> —vv. 24-25

THE REFORMATION SOCIETY OF JERUSALEM, 626 B.C.

Josiah's name is justly revered by all who love God's name. Yet we miss a vital feature of his achievement if we think he accomplished all this

by himself. Indeed, what sticks out about Josiah's reign and its after-
math is the many good and faithful men who supported the king, exe-
cuted his orders faithfully, and maintained the cause of reformation
long after his death.

It is important for us to realize that reformation does not rely only
on great figures. Certainly we should pray for a Jehoshaphat or Josiah
for our time, or if not them at least a modern-day Luther or Calvin. But
while we wait for dramatic intervention in our day, while we long for
God to raise up His Word once more in the hearts of His people, those
who seek reformation will join in the fray in whatever way God gives
them opportunity. So it was in the time of Josiah that God used a few
good men to make a great difference, to support the faithful king and
to carry on his work in darker days to come. Fittingly, their names
appear in conjunction with the return of God's Word:

> *When the king heard the words of the Book of the Law, he
> tore his clothes. And the king commanded Hilkiah the priest,
> and Ahikam the son of Shaphan, and Achbor the son of
> Micaiah, and Shaphan the secretary, and Asaiah the king's
> servant. . . .*
>
> —2 KINGS 22:11-12

These men were Josiah's assistants as the godly king pursued the difficult work of reformation, beginning in the year 626 B.C. What is so
striking is to see their presence felt much later in the midst of Jeremiah's
struggle with the wicked successors to the throne, around the year 590.
Jeremiah himself would have begun his ministry under the reign of
Josiah, and along with these officials he carried on the Lord's work in
the darkness that followed, in the last days before Jerusalem's fall.

In those late years Jeremiah bore the prophetic brunt of standing up
to the apostate kings. Jeremiah 26 tells of an attempt on his life by
Josiah's son, King Jehoiakim. Who was there to protect God's prophet
but the same Ahikam the son of Shaphan who so vitally supported King
Josiah! We are not told the details, only this: "But the hand of Ahikam
the son of Shaphan was with Jeremiah so that he was not given over to
the people to be put to death" (v. 24).

Later on Jeremiah sent his helper Baruch with a scroll to deliver the
Lord's message to the unbelieving king. Who was there but another

member of Shaphan's family, who like his fathers before him had entered into the cause of reformation: "When Micaiah the son of Gemariah, *son of Shaphan*, heard all the words of the Lord from the scroll, he went down to the king's house, into the secretary's chamber, and all the officials were sitting there" (36:11-12, emphasis added). Who were these officials but more members of the reformation party in Jerusalem? "Elishama the secretary, Delaiah the son of Shemaiah, Elnathan the son of Achbor, Gemariah the son of Shaphan, Zedekiah the son of Hananiah, and all the officials" (v. 12). Two of these men are positively identified as sons of two of Josiah's supporters, Achbor and Shaphan, and we may safely judge from the context that together they all formed a society working together for reformation. These men brought the scroll God had sent through Jeremiah, and they eagerly brought it before the evil king, seeking his conversion. How they must have shuddered with grief when callous Jehoiakim carved off the precious words into the fire one line at a time. And yet they kept their wits enough to be still of use. The passage ends by telling of King Jehoiakim's plot to take the prophet's life. But "the officials said to Baruch, 'Go and hide, you and Jeremiah, and let no one know where you are'" (36:19).

There are always little-known men and women of God who commit themselves to the faithful cause of reformation in the church. Their labors, even if unheralded, are precious to the Lord. God greatly used this group of committed reformers, even amidst the horrible judgment that fell upon Jerusalem with its destruction just a few years later, in 586 B.C. Their efforts failed in the world of men, but their names are recorded with honor in the Word of God. The flame of their works was all but snuffed out by mortal enemies, but God Himself tended to that flame to pass on their calling to other committed believers in every following generation. They lived in terrible times, but they made themselves available to the Lord and to His choice servants. And, significantly, they were still there after the compromising kings had been dragged off in chains. After Jerusalem was captured and occupied, it was one of this band—a man named Gedaliah son of Ahikam, yet another son of godly Shaphan, Josiah's secretary—whom the Babylonian governor placed in charge of the people left in the ruins of the city. God's faithful had survived the worst, they had persevered by God's grace, and they still were there as leaders for God to employ as shepherds over His scattered flock.

There are always little-known men and women whose labors,
even if unheralded, are precious to the Lord. The flame of the
works of this group of committed reformers was all but snuffed
out by mortal enemies, but God Himself tended to that flame
to pass on their calling to other committed believers in every
generation.

A FEW GOOD MEN

Church history records in every period of reformation that the church is
restored to purity and gospel power not merely through the great lights
whose names glitter on pages of sermons and books, but by a movement
of men and women inspired by God's Spirit and guided by His Word.
This is what we are called to today, whether our ministry is great or small.
Not only are we to serve the Lord in obedience, but to band together like
those men of old to contend for the faith. This is why Jude wrote of his
great concern for the early church, equally in need of reform:

> *Beloved, although I was very eager to write to you about our*
> *common salvation, I found it necessary to write appealing to*
> *you to contend for the faith that was once for all delivered to*
> *the saints.*
>
> —JUDE 3

Like us, Jude would have preferred to have given his attention to a
more positive mission, to exult in the joys of salvation together with
God's people. Yet his duty to Christ compelled him to write about the
need for reformation in his day. A great legacy had been entrusted to him
and to others; there had been a great formative work in the missionary
age of Christ's own apostles, and immediately there was a calling to contend for that faith that now was entrusted to the generation of believers
serving in the church. "Contend for the faith," he exhorts in the plural—
to all his readers—"that was once for all delivered to the saints."

This is our reply to all who scoff at a call for reformation, to those
who clamor for only encouraging reports, to those who cry out, "Peace,
peace" when there is no peace. God's Word itself commands us to contend for the treasure of the faith entrusted once and for all to the saints.

Jude's letter provides an outstanding model and agenda for believers today who would stand for Christ in the cause of reformation:

> *But you must remember, beloved, the predictions of the apostles of our Lord Jesus Christ. They said to you, "In the last time there will be scoffers, following their own ungodly passions." It is these who cause divisions, worldly people, devoid of the Spirit.*
>
> —vv. 17-19

Jude applied that prophecy to his own time, and we are to do the same; it certainly presents an admirable summary of what the church is facing today. What follows is a task that is ever urgent, and especially so when the church has gone astray:

> *But you, beloved, build yourselves up in your most holy faith; pray in the Holy Spirit; keep yourselves in the love of God, waiting for the mercy of our Lord Jesus Christ that leads to eternal life. And have mercy on those who doubt; save others by snatching them out of the fire; to others show mercy with fear, hating even the garment stained by the flesh.*
>
> —vv. 20-23

Lest we think this advocates a quiet pietism that avoids the demands of reformation, we should realize that all of these verbs are plural—they are for the church together and not just for individuals. Nor should we think this an agenda merely for missionary work in a non-Christian culture, for the context spoken of here is the church. Rather than abandon the church, as some would have us do, we must labor for the truth in the church. We could hardly do better than to take these words to heart, praying over them to God, that we might understand how He would have us stand in our own time, contending alongside other reformers for the faith entrusted to us for the sake of those who will follow.

The comparison between Josiah's time and our own is not one that is apparent to everyone. No smoke arises from pagan fires burning outside the walls of our churches. Yet the idols are there, with the values and principles and aspirations of the world, the tolerance for sin, the neglect of true and reverent biblical worship. Has the Bible been lost today as it was before the time of Josiah? The Bibles are there in our pews, but the place of God's Word has indeed been lost in the church as surely as if it were gathering dust in a corner of the temple. No longer is there confidence about its clarity to guide or its authority to rule, nor an understanding of its message. Behind all these symptoms today, as in the days when the boy-king came to his throne, is an indifference to God in the midst of our frenzied pursuit of self. As David Wells has observed, evangelicalism today is plagued by "the weightlessness" of its conception of God, so that things of God and of heaven are deemed irrelevant to the church, which instead draws its guidance from the priestly cult of secular psychologists.[1]

> *Evangelicalism today is plagued by "the weightlessness" of God, so that things of heaven are deemed irrelevant to the church, which having displaced God's Word draws its guidance from the priestly cult of secular psychologists.*

Our generation, like Josiah's, must discover the Bible anew, opening and reading the words of God's covenant book, seeing and understanding what God is about and what worship He demands. If we will turn to God's Word in earnest, gazing upon His perfect Law and Gospel, surely we will tear our clothes and come before the Lord in the grief of repentance, crying out, "Let us inquire of the Lord to see what He would have us do!" When that is done, we will find plenty of work for us all, as well as the opposition that always arises against biblical reformation in the church. Just as in days of old, there will be need for more than a few good men who want to serve the Lord.

> *Our generation, like Josiah's, must discover the Bible anew, seeing and understanding what God is about and what worship He demands, crying out, "Let us inquire of the Lord to see what He would have us do!"*

9

REFORMATION IN GALATIA

The purpose of this book is to examine the Bible's own mandate for reformation, looking mainly at material from the Old Testament. However, in order to show that what we have seen in Old Testament Israel carries over into the age of the church, this chapter considers the New Testament example of the apostle Paul in his letters to the churches. Paul's epistles were written for a variety of purposes. Romans was written to a church Paul had yet to visit; there we can read Paul's systematic gospel presentation. Ephesians sets forth advanced-level doctrine for the church, and in Philippians Paul writes to thank the Christians there for their care and concern, and to encourage them in the joy they ought to have as believers. Several of Paul's letters, however, stand out for their reforming intent, including his letters of pastoral instruction to Timothy and Titus, his first letter to the Corinthians, and his epistle to the churches in Galatia.

Our Old Testament studies revealed a clear pattern of formation-deformation-reformation. First there is *formation*. This is what took place in the Old Testament when Moses led Israel out of Egypt and finally brought them as a nation to the Promised Land; the book of Deuteronomy especially describes and records this formation. In the New Testament the same thing took place through the apostolic missions that formed the first churches. However, after formation comes *deformation*, as Israel and also the early churches fell under various influences and wandered from the path, sometimes in minor ways and sometimes decisively. *Reformation*, therefore, is the labor to reestablish first principles, to re-form the community of faith upon the instructions laid down by God through the prophets and apostles. Formation-deformation-reformation. That is the pattern we find in the experience of the prophets and apostles, and it is what we also wrestle with today.

FORMATION AND DEFORMATION IN GALATIA

One of the clearest examples of reformation in the New Testament church is the response of the apostle Paul to the doctrinal and practical deviations that set in among the churches of Galatia. Our source for this is Paul's great epistle to the Galatians, a letter that is noteworthy for its severity as well as for its doctrinal clarity. Instead of his normally cheery greeting, Paul addressed the situation with the ominous words, "I am astonished that you are so quickly deserting him who called you in the grace of Christ and are turning to a different gospel—not that there is another one, but there are some who trouble you and want to distort the gospel of Christ" (1:6-7).

The Galatian churches were formed by Paul and Barnabas during their first missionary journey, probably around the year A.D. 48. These are the churches we read about in Acts 13—14, located in what is now south-central Turkey. The historical record of the Galatian Christian churches begins rather momentously in Acts 13:14-16, where we read:

> They went on from Perga and came to Antioch in Pisidia. And on the Sabbath day they went into the synagogue and sat down. After the reading from the Law and the Prophets, the rulers of the synagogue sent a message to them, saying, "Brothers, if you have any word of exhortation for the people, say it." So Paul stood up, and motioning with his hand said: "Men of Israel and you who fear God, listen."

Thus was established Paul's church-planting strategy. He and Barnabas would go to the Jewish synagogue, where they would preach about Jesus Christ and form a group of converts. Paul built these churches not on the basis of his own dynamic personality, not by means of social events geared to make people think of Christianity as something fun, not by trying to meet people's felt needs in order to prove the relevance of the Gospel. What Paul preached was the Gospel itself—that is, the redemptive work of God in history focused on the life, death, and resurrection of Jesus Christ for the forgiveness of our sins.

Paul built these churches not on the basis of his own dynamic personality, not by means of social events geared to make people think of Christianity as something fun, not by trying to meet people's felt needs in order to prove the relevance of the Gospel. Paul preached the Gospel of forgiveness for our sins.

In Acts 13:38 Paul sums up his message: "Let it be known to you therefore, brothers, that through this man forgiveness of sins is proclaimed to you." Paul's proclamation was one that dealt with man's condemnation before God on account of sin, the remedy of which was Christ's saving work alone.

The kind of preaching we read about in Acts 13 caused quite a stir. Two things resulted: a body of new believers and persecution, mainly from Jews who rejected Paul's message. That is what we see all through the formation of these churches in Acts 13—14: Paul and Barnabas preached the Gospel of salvation from sin and condemnation through Jesus Christ. Sometimes their message was accompanied by signs and miracles, which served not to replace but to validate their message (Acts 14:3); but the clear emphasis was on the proclamation of the Gospel itself. This is what we see in each of the Galatian cities mentioned in Acts: Pisidian Antioch, Iconium, Lystra, and Derbe. Acts 14:21-23 tells us how this first missionary journey wrapped up, after which Paul and Barnabas returned to Antioch and then went down to Jerusalem:

When they had preached the gospel to that city [Derbe] and had made many disciples, they returned to Lystra and to Iconium and to Antioch, strengthening the souls of the disciples, encouraging them to continue in the faith, and saying that through many tribulations we must enter the kingdom of God. And when they had appointed elders for them in every church, with prayer and fasting they committed them to the Lord in whom they had believed.

Thus was completed the formation of the churches in Galatia.

Paul's letter to the Galatians seems to have been written not long after this, perhaps after he had returned to Jerusalem in A.D. 49 or shortly beforehand. There are a number of reasons for this chronology, which is somewhat debated by scholars. In Galatians 1:6 we see that it could not have been written much after Paul's own ministry there because he says, "I am astonished that you are so quickly deserting him who called you in the grace of Christ and are turning to a different gospel." The key expression is "so quickly," which tells us that what Paul is writing about happened shortly after he departed. Another good reason for such an early dating is that Paul's concerns in this letter closely match those discussed in the Council of Jerusalem in Acts 15—namely, whether or not Gentile converts needed to be circumcised and to follow the Law of Moses. That conference took place in A.D. 49, after Paul's return from his ministry in Galatia. By this reckoning, Galatians is probably the first of the New Testament books to be written.

These churches had been founded by the great apostle Paul himself. The same Paul who wrote Romans and Ephesians was teaching them, forming them into a body, choosing, preparing, and ordaining elders to lead them. And yet in so short a time they had fallen away so badly that Paul was tempted to despair of them altogether. In Galatians 4:11 he writes, "I am afraid I may have labored over you in vain." This should give some perspective on the struggles we face today; if this could happen to Paul, it is no shock if we experience similar struggles.

These churches had been founded by the great apostle Paul himself: teaching them, forming them into a body, choosing, preparing, and ordaining elders to lead them. And yet in so short a time they had fallen away so badly that Paul was tempted to despair of them altogether.

THE PROBLEM OF FALSE TEACHERS

What were the problems in Galatia? What was the deformation that followed so quickly on the heels of Paul's formative ministry? We do not have to read far in Galatians to get quite a bit of insight on this matter. In verse 7 of chapter 1 Paul writes, "There are some who trouble you and want to distort the gospel of Christ."

This gives us our first point when it comes to understanding deformation as it is presented in the New Testament: namely, *it is the result of the work of false teachers.* This is the kind of thing we don't like to discuss today. We don't like to accept the possibility, much less any actual evidence, that there are false teachers in our midst. But such an idea was not at all difficult for Paul to swallow. We think, for instance, of his warning to the Ephesian elders in Acts 20:

> *"I know that after my departure fierce wolves will come in among you, not sparing the flock; and from among your own selves will arise men speaking twisted things, to draw away the disciples after them. Therefore be alert, remembering that for three years I did not cease night or day to admonish everyone with tears."*
>
> —vv. 29-31

In Paul's view, it is ludicrous *not* to think there will be enemies of the church who seek to work from within, primarily from positions of leadership. Indeed, one of Satan's primary means of attacking the church is to send false teachers. That will seem harsh to some people. But remember the parable Jesus told in Matthew 13:

> *"The kingdom of heaven may be compared to a man who sowed good seed in his field, but while his men were sleeping, his enemy came and sowed weeds among the wheat and went away. So when the plants came up and bore grain, then the weeds appeared also. And the servants of the master of the house came and said to him, 'Master, did you not sow good seed in your field? How then does it have weeds?' He said to them, 'An enemy has done this.'"*
>
> —vv. 24-28

There is an enemy who works by means of infiltration into the ranks of the church, where he can sow bad seed and entangle the people of God. As we look in the New Testament, this is a key source of deformation. This is not merely Paul's idea but also that of the other apostles. Peter's second epistle is largely devoted to this topic. Using the example of Israel to warn his own readers, he says, "False prophets also arose among the people, just as there will be false teachers among you, who will secretly bring in destructive heresies, even denying the Master who bought them, bringing upon themselves swift destruction. And many will follow their sensuality, and because of them the way of truth will be blasphemed" (2 Pet. 2:1-2). That is a veritable history of deformation in all ages, including our own. The apostle John is even stronger in what he says about this, writing in 2 John:

For many deceivers have gone out into the world, those who do not confess the coming of Jesus Christ in the flesh. Such a one is the deceiver and the antichrist. Watch yourselves, so that you may not lose what we have worked for, but may win a full reward. Everyone who goes on ahead and does not abide in the teaching of Christ, does not have God. Whoever abides in the teaching has both the Father and the Son. If anyone comes to you and does not bring this teaching, do not receive him into your house or give him any greeting, for whoever greets him takes part in his wicked works.

—vv. 7-11

John has particular heresies in mind, but the problem he sees is the same as that spoken against by Paul and Peter—namely, false teachers infiltrating and deforming the church. Indeed, according to Paul's warning in Acts 20, a failure to accept this and guard against it with vigor constitutes culpable negligence on the part of the elders and shepherds of the flock. We will see a similar emphasis when our study proceeds to Jesus' letters to the churches in Revelation.

According to the New Testament, deformation is the result of the work of false teachers. Failure to guard against this constitutes culpable negligence on the part of the elders and shepherds of the flock.

In Paul's opposition to false teachers he is connected to a strand that runs all through the Bible. We remember Samuel debating those who wanted a human king like that of the nations. We think of the false prophets who proffered false peace to the wicked kings in the time of Jeremiah and who in their great multitude applauded the strategies of Ahab. In so many ways the tale of deformation and reformation is that of the false prophets against the true.

The second thing we see about the deformation in Galatia is *the method of false teachers*—namely, the adding of human teaching, human insight, and human wisdom to the teaching of God's Word that came by revelation through the apostle. Paul makes quite a point of this, as we see in Galatians 1:11-12: "For I would have you know, brothers, that the gospel that was preached by me is not man's gospel. For I did not receive it from any man, nor was I taught it, but I received it through a revelation of Jesus Christ."

Deformation proceeds along the highway of human insight and invention, teachings that came not from God but from the hearts and minds of men. In Galatia this took the form of a Jewish legalism that insisted that faith in Christ be accompanied by a reliance on the Law for justification. To be right with God, these false teachers said, you have to be circumcised and you have to follow the law with its dietary restrictions, cleanliness laws, etc. That made sense to them from their Jewish perspective; it was important according to their wisdom. With human insight they utterly perverted the Gospel; but if they were right, Paul noted, "Christ died for no purpose" (Gal. 2:21).

Deformation proceeds along the highway of human insight and invention, teachings that came not from God but from the hearts and minds of men.

The same thing happened in Corinth, but the particular form that the wisdom of men assumed there was somewhat different. There it was not Judaism that was intruding on the Gospel but Greek philosophy. The false teachers deforming that church were not trying to please the Jews but the Greeks, and they attacked the Gospel not because of the scandal of its cross but for the foolishness of its philosophy.

This is how deformation works today as well, through human wisdom that perverts the Gospel given from God by revelation. Of course, I do not know anybody who argues the need for circumcision, and I seldom hear Greek philosophy as an objection to the Gospel today. Neither of those, of course, are the wisdom of our day. What is the wisdom of our day? Tolerance, doubt, relativism, utilitarianism. And our false teachers trumpet these as loudly as the Judaizers and the rhetoricians of Corinth ever voiced their attacks on the Gospel.

Consider this objection to historic Christianity: "So much has changed since the Bible was written. We are so far removed culturally and historically, and our situation is so very different from theirs! We cannot be expected to apply this teaching at face value." That is what you hear from the false teachers of today, many in evangelical garb, espousing their human insight and imposing their ideas upon the church and its view of Scripture. And yet what really has changed? Is man less sinful, is guilt less damning, is God less holy, is Christ less sufficient to save? Nothing of real consequence has changed since Paul first revealed the Gospel in the synagogues of those Galatian cities. What Christianity deals with is God and eternity, about which we know nothing apart from revelation, and upon the understanding of which our own wisdom and insight exerts an influence that is only corrupting. We must be conformed to God's revelation, and not the other way around. If we are to receive the Gospel from God, then we must neither add to it nor subtract from it. *This* must be our response to the false teachers of today.

What is the wisdom of our day? Tolerance, doubt, relativism, utilitarianism. And the false teachers today trumpet these as loudly as the Judaizers and the rhetoricians of Corinth ever voiced their attacks on the Gospel.

There is always a temptation toward relying on human wisdom in the academic community, and it is for this reason that deformation often comes from the seminaries and universities. The temptation is to make the Bible the domain of specialists, its interpretation a matter of investigative methods inaccessible to the simple man or woman unskilled in scholastic tools and methods. When we start thinking this way, we always stop receiving the Scripture as the Word of God who communicates to us with clarity. The Bible becomes arcane, and specialist scholars become priestly interpreters who tell us what they have unearthed and discovered. We should not be at all opposed to scholarship, as long as scholars take the Bible as God's revealed Word to be received by faith and not something determined by scholarly works. Martyn Lloyd-Jones saw this as a great concern a generation ago, arguing that Scripture should be received as revealed from God, and not as reconstructed by human inquiry. He said:

> The gospel which I am privileged to preach to you is primarily a matter of revelation. It is not enquiry, it is not discovery. More or less everything else in life is enquiry and discovery, that is why we drop into that habit, and think it should apply here. Is that not the argument of the modern man; he says all truth is discovered in science and nature as the result of investigation, why not here? The answer is that here you start with revelation not investigation, a

man by searching cannot 'find out God' (Job 11:7). . . . This Christian faith is not philosophy, it is not what men think of God and life and the world; it is God revealing himself, God coming to us and telling us things, it is revelation. That is the reason we must not come in the spirit of investigation and examination; here is revelation to which we must look and listen.[1]

Academic humanism is one source of false teaching, but another is the pragmatism that comes from the workplace. It makes sense to bring wisdom that is effective in business into the church, and yet to do so is to create a new and different gospel. Certainly we may have good ideas from the business world or the military or the media, but they must all be checked with and controlled by the Word of God, by the Gospel revealed in Scripture with its logic and its means and its ends. Otherwise deformation proceeds naturally from the incorporation of human wisdom and insight into the holy precincts of the church.

This is what caused the problem in Galatia: new teachings that were from man and not from God by revelation. Paul's unmistakable point in Galatians 1 is that mixing the Word of God with the wisdom of man produces a different gospel altogether, indeed one that is no gospel at all; it produces confusion and perverts the Gospel of Christ (Gal. 1:6-7).

On Ends and Means

Paul goes on to tell us about the *motives or the agenda of the false teachers*, writing in 4:17 of the ends they sought and the means they employed: "They make much of you, but for no good purpose. They want to shut you out, that you may make much of them."

In other words, they were trying to build their own following. Paul says in Galatians 4:19 that his own goal is that Christ would be formed in them, while the false teachers were merely trying to swell their own power base.

There is a world of difference between forming disciples for Christ and winning converts to your own cause, your own church, your own ministry. The difference is one we encountered before—namely, between thinking of people as sinners who need to be saved versus consumers you are trying to convert into customers. That is quite a difference of agenda, and it explains how deformation consistently works.

There is a world of difference between forming disciples for Christ and winning converts to your own ministry, between thinking of people as sinners who need to be saved versus consumers you are trying to convert into customers.

That difference will manifest itself both in the ends we pursue and the means we employ. In what was Paul interested? What were the ends toward which he formed these churches? If we are at all familiar with his letters, the answer is obvious. Paul's goal was the salvation of sinners and the glory of God. Going back to Galatians 4:19, Paul addresses "my little children, for whom I am again in the anguish of childbirth until Christ is formed in you." He wants their salvation both *from* the bondage and condemnation of sin and *to* the freedom that is found in the Gospel. That is one of his great ends. But there is another that is, if anything, even more important to Paul. It is with this that he closes his epistle: "But far be it from me to boast except in the cross of our Lord Jesus Christ, by which the world has been crucified to me, and I to the world" (6:14). That was his boast and his goal—the cross and its power and its salvation and its God and Savior. We see the same in Paul's letters to the Corinthians, where he sums up his desire by an appeal to Jeremiah 9:23: "Let the one who boasts, boast in the Lord" (1 Cor. 1:31). In all this he is pointedly confronting the motives of his rivals who promoted deformation.

You can always tell what people value by listening to what they talk about. Paul's letters are not about what is going on in the world, what will impress Caesar, how to make a better impression or gather greater worldly power. His prayers, especially, tell us where his heart is. He prays that the Ephesians would know God better and understand the riches of their salvation (1:16-21). In Philippians Paul thanks God for their faith (1:3-5). In Colossians he writes, "We always thank God, the Father of our Lord Jesus Christ, when we pray for you, since we heard of your faith in Christ Jesus and of the love that you have for all the saints, because of the hope laid up for you in heaven" (1:3-5). Those were the things Paul was excited to see—the Gospel bearing fruit in lives of faith. Perhaps his greatest obsession, in which these are all summed up, is revealed in Romans 11:33-36: "Oh, the depth of the riches and wisdom and knowledge of God! How unsearchable are his judgments and how inscrutable his ways! . . . For from him and through him and to him are all things. To him be glory forever. Amen. "

You can always tell what people value by listening to what they talk about. Paul prayed that Christians would know God better and understand the riches of their salvation. Those were the things Paul was excited to see—the Gospel bearing fruit in lives of faith.

Since those were Paul's objectives, his means were chosen appropriately. To glorify God he used the means given by God. To lead people to faith in the Christ of the Gospel, he made the Gospel itself his instrument. When people didn't like it—as often happened—he did not mold his message according to their consumer tastes. Instead, he warned them of the judgment awaiting those who reject God's Gospel (see Acts 13:40). When the Jews in Galatia began persecuting Paul and Barnabas, those men of God did not change their tune but boldly answered their critics, "It was necessary that the word of God be spoken first to you. Since you thrust it aside and judge yourselves unworthy of eternal life, behold, we are turning to the Gentiles" (Acts 13:46).

To glorify God Paul used the means given by God. To lead people to faith in the Christ of the Gospel, he made the Gospel itself his instrument.

The false teachers of Galatia had a very different agenda, with different ends and different means. They wanted to win consumers over to themselves as customers. This is what we see today, with what I have heard referred to as the ABC's of church success: attendance, buildings, and cash. All of these can be had without the Gospel; indeed, it is easier to achieve such goals with a soothing therapeutic message than with the hard-edged Word of God.

Consumerism fashions its goods and services according to the tastes of the buyers. Here persuasion depends upon the will of the hearer and not on the grace of a sovereign God. It is no surprise to find that perhaps the two chief tenets of modern church growth theory are accommodation to the preferences of seekers and the blasphemous idea that "the audience is sovereign." Such an approach to religion brings glory to man—to the preacher and to the good people who signed on—rather than to God alone. Since Paul was a threat to them, the false teachers strongly attacked Paul's credentials and ministry in order to loosen the young churches' loyalty to him. "Those people are zealous to win you over, but for no good. What they want is to alienate you from us, so that you may be zealous for them," he writes (4:17, NIV).

In Galatians 6:12-13 Paul adds to his assessment of the false teachers' motives, and what he says fits the profile we have already developed:

> *It is those who want to make a good showing in the flesh who would force you to be circumcised, and only in order that they may not be persecuted for the cross of Christ. For even those who are circumcised do not themselves keep the law, but they desire to have you circumcised that they may boast in your flesh.*

Here is an important statement regarding the agenda of the false teachers. It was true in Galatia, and it was true in Corinth. A reliance on human wisdom, human methods, for the attainment of results that are impressive to the world ultimately constitutes a betrayal of the cross. This was part of the whole program in Galatia, as it was in Corinth. An appeal to worldly logic—Jewish legalism in Galatia and Greek sophistication in Corinth—masked an unwillingness to stand before the world with the cross that it hates. To trust worldly methods is to deny the sufficiency of faith for salvation; to smuggle in human ability and merit into the formula of salvation is to render Christ's death pointless.

When Paul says the false teachers are seeking to avoid persecution for the sake of the cross, he reminds us that it is the cross that makes people antagonistic toward Christianity. The cross tells the man on the street that he is not basically good, that his guilt demands a sacrifice that he himself cannot offer, that he needs a substitute, even the perfect Son of God. The cross tells proud people that they had better humble themselves, confess their total failure and profound guilt, and place all their hope in the blood of Jesus Christ. It is to this that Paul himself clings, in contrast to his opponents. They want "to boast in your flesh," he claims (Gal. 6:13), not about your faith in Christ but in your works of the law. "Far be it from me to boast," Paul replies in deliberate contrast, "except in the cross of our Lord Jesus Christ, by which the world has been crucified to me, and I to the world" (6:14).

It is the cross that makes people antagonistic toward Christianity. The cross tells the man on the street that he is not basically good, that his guilt demands a sacrifice he himself cannot offer, that he needs a substitute, even the perfect Son of God.

In review of Paul's opposition, how familiar this all is to us today. False teachers speak in the name of Christ while they build their own empires on the basis of consumerism, as they compete with other leaders for control of the masses, armed with a logic not from God but one that appeals to the outward sense of man. Now, as then, the end of such is a boasting in the flesh and a denial of the cross, which is our only hope in life and death.

PAUL'S REFORMING AGENDA

This brings us to Paul's response in terms of reformation. We find the same things that infected the Galatians in our own midst, in our own churches, and we ask, "What is the biblical model for leadership that reforms?" In the Old Testament we considered the examples of Jehoshaphat and Josiah. Now in the New Testament we see in Paul's response to the Galatians a similar approach that gives clarity to our task today.

Paul's response in Galatians reveals a four-point agenda for reformation. First, we see *the vigor with which he opposes false teachers.* To say the least, Paul's response to them is direct and uncompromising. He does not look for things he can compliment them about, he does not ease his way into criticism, but he treats them as enemies of the Gospel. As a good shepherd, his first thought is not for his own reputation—and standing up to false teachers always costs you in this department—not for what others would think, not for the trouble his stand will cost him. Rather, his thought is for the sheep. He wants to warn them about wolves, and he does this by first identifying the wolves as such.

Every time a church body ordains a man to the ministry, it exercises a solemn obligation to protect the weak and vulnerable lambs of Christ. This does not mean we should treat people with suspicion or belligerence. We simply should be watchful; we should jealously guard the teaching office of Christ's church. We can oppose false teaching without being cantankerous and mean-spirited, and we can identify those who lead the flock astray as wolves and false teachers without being malicious. Indeed, it is our duty to identify them and to do so publicly if necessary.

> We should treat people without suspicion or belligerence, jeal-ously guarding the teaching office of Christ's church. We can oppose false teaching without being mean-spirited, and we can identify those who lead the flock astray as false teachers with-out being malicious.

Look at what Paul says in Galatians 1:9: "As we have said before, so now I say again: If anyone is preaching to you a gospel contrary to the one you received, let him be accursed." Those are strong words, but they show us his attitude toward heretics. In Galatians 5:12 he gets even stronger. Speaking about his opponents' obsession with circumcision, he writes, "I wish those who unsettle you would emasculate themselves!"

Surely some qualifications are in order here. Paul, as an apostle, may speak with greater harshness than is perhaps appropriate for the rest of us. Furthermore, it is always a great victory for Satan when we take this need for watchfulness and make it our primary business. It is not our main business, and it should never be our passion. Our greatest task is the work of the Gospel itself for the glory of God, the salvation of sin-ners, and the building up of the church. We must avoid the extremes, both negligence and a culture of suspicion, which do great harm to the church.

What is most striking of all is not what Paul says about the false teachers, but what he writes about the apostle Peter in chapter 2 of Galatians. He recalls an incident that happened in the past, when he and Barnabas were ministering among the Gentiles in Antioch. Peter came up and freely joined in the fellowship until a delegation from Jerusalem arrived, after which Peter stopped publicly associating with Gentiles at their dinner table. The issue, of course, was ceremonial cleanliness under the Law. Not only did Paul publicly stand up to Peter himself, calling him a hypocrite—*the* Simon Peter, *the* chief apostle—but he later writes about it in this public document.

> But when Cephas came to Antioch, I opposed him to his face, because he stood condemned. . . . But when I saw that their conduct was not in step with the truth of the gospel, I said to Cephas before them all, "If you, though a Jew, live like a

Gentile and not like a Jew, how can you force the Gentiles to live like Jews?"

—vv. 11-14

That passage reveals a radical commitment to truth that we cannot ignore. Paul's attitude is so very different from our own, and yet we see it again in other great reforming leaders. John Calvin, for instance, showed a striking determination to oppose and expose error. Speaking on Paul's attitude in 2 Timothy 2:16-18, where the apostle identifies false teachers by name, Calvin writes:

> We see the flock of God troubled and tormented with ravenous wolves, that devour and destroy whatsoever they can. Must we be moved with mercy towards a wolf; and in the meantime let the poor sheep and lambs of which our Lord hath such a special care, let them, I say, perish? When we see any wicked man troubling the church either by offenses or false doctrine, we must prevent him as much as lies in our power; we must warn the simple, that they be not misled and carried away; this I say, is our duty. The Lord would have the wicked made known, that the world may discern them, that their ungodliness may be made manifest to all. . . . When we see them thus, must we hold our peace? Let us learn to know them that trouble the church of God, and keep them back, and endeavor to prevent them from doing injury. Hereby we see how few there are that have a zeal for God's church.[2]

Indeed we do. One of the important duties of a preacher is to refute error. It is not a preacher's only duty, and it certainly should never be his main preoccupation or joy. You find people with that kind of critical and threatening attitude toward every point of disagreement, and they too are a menace to the church. But Paul's attitude is very instructive. For Paul, the truth was vitally important. He was willing to jeopardize relationships and reputations, if he had to, but he was determined to uphold the truth of the Gospel because a failure to do so jeopardizes the church. The first thing we observe about Paul, then, is his fierce opposition to false teachers.

The second thing that characterizes Paul's reforming response is his application of a great principle of the Bible, one that is very important to the Old Testament message and is equally valid in the New. This is the second plank of his reforming platform—*the assertion of Scripture's authority and sufficiency.*

In our study of the man of God from Judah we examined the biblical qualifications of a prophet. The mark of a true prophet was that he taught in conformity to what had already been revealed in Scripture, since all prior revelation is normative and binding for future revelation. According to this principle, any new message that contradicts the old message is false and must be rejected. This speaks of the authority, the binding character, of the revealed Word of God.

This is an important part of Paul's argument against the false teachers of Galatia. He writes in 1:8-9, "But even if we or an angel from heaven should preach to you a gospel contrary to the one we preached to you, let him be accursed. As we have said before, so now I say again: If anyone is preaching to you a gospel contrary to the one you received, let him be accursed." What Paul is saying is a vital principle for our own time as well. Once God has spoken by revelation, and that is what He did during Paul's ministry in Galatia, then anyone else, even if it is an angel, even if Paul himself were to come back with a contradictory message from what God has authoritatively revealed through Paul's apostolic preaching, must be rejected and treated as one who is under God's condemnation.

That is the second emphasis Paul shows in Galatians. First he opposes false teachers, along with their methods and message. Second, he asserts the vital principle of the binding character of prior revelation.

The third thing Paul did was to *correct error with apostolic teaching as revealed by God.* All through the letter to the Galatians, but especially in chapters 3 and 4, Paul addressed himself to the errors and countered them with clear, compelling, and pointed biblical teaching. In chapter 3 he argues that the Galatians did not originally receive God's Spirit through the Law but through faith in the message about Christ. Then he used the example of Abraham as our father—not his law-keeping but his faith. Then he pointed out that Christ is the seed of Abraham spoken of in Genesis, whose coming ends the time of pedagogy. In chapter 4 Paul employs the illustration of a slave in contrast to a child, developing this by means of the contrast between Hagar and Sarah. All of this represents a major and essential aspect of his reforming program— namely, thorough and doctrinal Bible teaching.

There was a great difference between Paul's mode of teaching and that of the false teachers. Paul did not repackage his message to make it more competitive and attractive vis-a-vis the false teachers. He did not appeal to human ways of thinking but to the text of the Scriptures and the interpretation revealed by God. He did not dress up the message to make it more relevant. The Gospel *is* relevant; it is always relevant, as long as there are sinners, as long as God sits upon a holy throne of judgment, as long as lawbreakers are under the condemnation and in the bondage of sin. The Gospel is relevant to the ultimate and greatest needs of every man and woman, needs that do not change with the generations or intellectual fashions. Paul vigorously and systematically taught the Gospel from the text of the Scripture.

The Gospel is relevant, as long as there are sinners, as long as God sits upon a holy throne of judgment, as long as sinners are under the condemnation and in the bondage of sin. The Gospel is relevant to the ultimate and greatest needs, which do not change with the generations or intellectual fashions.

Fourth and finally, *Paul directed his readers toward authentic biblical spirituality.* The Judaizers taught an inauthentic and false spirituality based on human attainment and law-keeping. Paul's great response is in Galatians 2:19-20: "I have been crucified with Christ. It is no longer I who live, but Christ who lives in me. And the life I now live in the flesh I live by faith in the Son of God, who loved me and gave himself for me."

Faith in Christ has radical implications, and Paul presses them upon the deformed churches of Galatia. Do not accept the bondage of human programs and enslaving methodologies, he says. Yet is that not the dominant mode of spirituality today? Join this discipleship program; buy this product; fast; pray; engage in this discipline. These things may be good; certainly prayer is essential to true spirituality, as we have seen. But none of these can replace a personal reliance on the grace of God as offered in the Gospel of Christ. Paul's spirituality depended on a message, not a method; he said, "For freedom Christ has set us free; stand firm therefore, and do not submit again to a yoke of slavery" (5:1).

Paul wants the kind of spirituality that flows from faith in Christ, from reliance on His finished achievement and the Holy Spirit's work within us. What counts, he says in Galatians 5:6, is "faith working through love." That is what faith produces, the fulfillment of the great commandment given through Moses in Deuteronomy and repeated by Jesus:

*And he said to him, "You shall love the Lord your God with all
your heart and with all your soul and with all your mind. This
is the great and first commandment. And a second is like it: You
shall love your neighbor as yourself. On these two commandments depend all the Law and the Prophets."*

—MATT. 22:37-40

In other words, according to Paul, true spirituality is biblical living,
the very kind set forth so long ago in Deuteronomy. Moses said,
"Circumcise therefore the foreskin of your heart, and be no longer stubborn" (Deut. 10:16). "But I say," Paul writes in Galatians 5:16, "walk
by the Spirit, and you will not gratify the desires of the flesh." Authentic
biblical spirituality is inseparable from faith in the work of Jesus Christ
and obedience to the Word of God. "Do not be conformed to this
world," Paul writes in Romans 12:2, "but be transformed by the
renewal of your mind."

Just as we must teach the Gospel, we must also lead the body of
Christ in the way of the true Christian life. Reformation may begin with
opposition to false teachers and error in the church; it may and always
does require a reassertion of biblical authority and sufficiency. But all
this serves the greater end of a recommitment to the Lord Himself and
the living implications of a whole reliance on the sufficient work of
Christ as our Savior.

Paul's letters do not show us his whole ministry. But they do reveal a
fervent life of prayer, just like the reformers of the Old Testament, as well
as a significant concern over the reform of worship and practical mercy
within the church. But blazing through all his letters is his great passion
for a message that changed his life. At the heart of his reforming message
to the Galatians is this powerful testimony of what the Gospel had done
to him: "I died to the law, so that I might live to God. I have been crucified with Christ. It is no longer I who live, but Christ who lives in me. And
the life I now live in the flesh I live by faith in the Son of God, who loved
me and gave himself for me" (Gal. 2:19-20). May God grant us grace to
recover such a passion for so great a saving God, who is worthy of all our
lives, and such confidence in the Gospel, which is sufficient for the growth
and care and reformation of the church so dearly loved by our Lord.

10

CHRIST'S LETTER TO THE CHURCHES

If our survey of biblical material has not proved sufficient to establish both a mandate and a pattern for reformation, we come now to a concluding portion of Scripture that irrefutably presses these upon us. At the end of the Bible our Lord Jesus Christ appears risen and exalted in glory, standing amidst the lampstands as the Great Reformer of His church. In the book of Revelation we are confronted with Christ's final statement in Scripture to the churches. After these letters, the apostle John is brought into the consideration of great heavenly and future realities, and the Bible concludes with its glorious panorama of the eternal glory of heaven.

ONE LIKE A SON OF MAN

The sight of Jesus Christ is one that is welcome to His people. In Him all the problems of the Bible receive their answer. We think of the great drama of Jesus' appearance to Thomas, who refused to believe Jesus' resurrection unless he felt the marks on his hands and side. When our Lord appeared to Thomas and told him to put his finger into His wounds so he would believe, He was presenting God's solution to the sin of the world. Our thoughts travel back to the hillside of Mount Ebal, where the tribes of Israel spoke forth the curses from God on sin, and here is where those curses have landed. Paul explains, "Christ redeemed us from the curse of the law by becoming a curse for us" (Gal. 3:13). This informs us that the answer to the sinner's need of redemption and to the church's great problem of deformation is found in the person and work of Jesus Christ

Himself. "He died for all, that those who live might no longer live for themselves but for him who for their sake died and was raised" (2 Cor. 5:15). Reformation relies on the death of Christ—for there our sin was taken away—as well as on His resurrection—for out of His everlasting life He has power to send to us the Holy Spirit for new repentance and faith. It is fitting, then, that our study of reformation leads us to the feet of the Lord Himself, risen and exalted with salvation for the church.

> *The answer to the great problem of deformation and sin is found in the person and work of Jesus Christ Himself. Reformation relies on His death and resurrection.*

What strikes us, therefore, when we are brought before Jesus in Revelation 1—3 for His message to the church is that He appears not so much as Savior but as Lord. He *is* our Savior, but here it is not the marks of our redemption that come to the fore, but rather His emblems of sovereignty, glory, and power.

The apostle John tells us he was in the Spirit when he heard a loud voice calling him to take a message to the churches:

> *Then I turned to see the voice that was speaking to me, and on turning I saw seven golden lampstands, and in the midst of the lampstands one like a son of man, clothed with a long robe and with a golden sash around his chest. The hairs of his head were white like wool, as white as snow. His eyes were like a flame of fire, his feet were like burnished bronze, refined in a furnace, and his voice was like the roar of many waters. In his right hand he held seven stars, from his mouth came a sharp two-edged sword, and his face was like the sun shining in full strength.*
>
> —REV. 1:12-16

John is brought to his Master the way Moses was brought to Mount Sinai, with a trumpet blast summoning him to divinity (v. 10; cf. Exod. 19:16, 19; 20:18). Like Ezekiel, the voice he heard was "like the sound of many waters, like the sound of the Almighty, a sound of tumult like the sound of an army" (Ezek. 1:24). Jesus' voice, so often heard at John's side during the Savior's life on earth, comes forth now as the voice of the Almighty. Jesus is "one like a son of man" (Rev. 1:13), an allusion to the vision of Daniel 7, dressed in the heavenly garb of the true high priest, with robe and golden sash (Exod. 28:4; 29:9). He is also the Great Prophet, with "a sharp two-edged sword" coming from his mouth (Rev. 1:16; cf. Isa. 49:2). John worships Him as the high and holy king, falling down like Isaiah as he senses his own defilement: "When I saw him, I fell at his feet as though dead" (Rev. 1:17; cf. Isa. 6:5). Jesus is the Lord Almighty, reigning in power in His threefold office of prophet, priest, and king.

This vision not only highlights the sovereign glory of Jesus in His exaltation, but also His present relationship to the church. John sees Him standing in the midst of seven golden lampstands (v. 13). In his right hand are seven stars, which, he says, "are the angels of the seven churches, and the seven lampstands are the seven churches" (v. 20). The seven letters that follow are each addressed "to the angel of the church" in that place. This may indicate the messenger entrusted with the message (*angel* means "messenger") or perhaps the pastor whom Jesus holds responsible for that church. But it is more likely that Jesus means a guardian angel charged with protecting God's people in a certain place, just as Daniel's prophecy spoke of guardian angels who served and protected Israel (Dan. 10:12-13). Dennis Johnson persuasively argues that "the stars symbolize angels, who in turn symbolize the churches," which makes sense in light of Jesus' clear intent to speak to the churches themselves.

The stars and lampstands also indicate the function of the churches. Johnson writes, "Stars and lampstands both speak of the churches as reflecting the light of their King, but the lampstands highlight his presence and the stars emphasize his protective possessiveness. The glorious Son of Man, who lives among his congregations and holds their lives in his hand, has something to say to each of them."[1] Here, then, is the picture: The exalted Christ is Lord Almighty of the church, among which He Himself walks, which He possesses and protects, and in which He seeks the manifestation of His own glorious light.

The exalted Christ is Lord Almighty of the church, among which He Himself walks, which He possesses and protects, and in which He seeks the manifestation of His own glorious light.

TO THE SEVEN CHURCHES

Jesus' appearance anticipates the content of the messages He will send. Jesus is Lord and King, and He demands the obedience of His church. His appearance and clothing speak of priestly holiness, and this He seeks in those who follow Him. From His mouth comes the sword of God's Word, and this He expects to see proclaimed, defended, and applied in the church. As He holds the churches in His hand, so too does He look to them to hold fast to Him as the light and the glory of the church. He holds, as He says to John in 1:18, "the keys of Death and Hades," and so He speaks to the church as One who can enforce His commands as well as reward those who serve Him in faith and love.

Before we turn to the content of these seven letters, we would do well to observe the example that Jesus, the Chief Shepherd, sets for all the under-shepherds who serve in His name. Jesus cares for His churches. He is interested and involved. Therefore, He shows detailed knowledge of their spiritual state; He says over and again, "I know." Vern S. Poythress observes that Christ addresses "each one according to its needs, with encouragement, rebuke, exhortation, and promise. . . . All the churches are caught up in a universal calling to faithfulness in the heavenly Jerusalem."[2] The number seven represents completeness and universality. So these churches stand for more than their own local conditions; they speak to churches of every place and every time. Jesus is therefore seen as the reforming Lord of His cherished church; it is from Him that pastors and other church leaders receive their mandate today for reforming ministries within His flock.

Jesus is the reforming Lord of His cherished church; it is from Him that pastors and other church leaders receive their mandate today for reforming ministries within His flock.

A survey of these seven letters reveals themes that are of demonstrated importance to our Lord. The first of these is the vital significance He assigns to the matter of truth in the church. His first letter praises the Ephesians for testing those falsely claiming to be apostles, as well as for opposing an otherwise unknown heresy of "the Nicolaitans" (2:2, 6). We are reminded here of the Deuteronomic requirement for testing false prophets; the Ephesians evidently succeeded where the man of God from

Judah failed. Dennis Johnson remarks, "The church's intolerance was as politically incorrect in the midst of ancient pluralism as it would be today; but it reflected Jesus' intolerance of poisonous lies and of liars who prey on his sheep."[3]

Jesus particularly takes note of this in the church at Pergamum, which holds fast to the truth in the face of deadly persecution (2:13). Nonetheless, it comes under His criticism for permitting false teaching that encourages licentiousness (which seems to be the point of "the teaching of Balaam") as well as the Nicolaitan heresy. It is noteworthy that while only some have gone in for these false teachings, the whole church is charged by our Lord for permitting it. Similarly, the church in Thyatira is charged for permitting a figure Jesus identifies as "that woman Jezebel," whose false teaching led to sexual immorality and idolatry (2:20).

Surely this tells us that we must disabuse ourselves of the possibility of neutrality when it comes to matters of truth. There are good reasons for us to avoid controversy; surely we should neither seek it nor love it. But we are called to realize that in a world such as ours, in a time like that in which we live, when truth is up for sale, there is no neutrality. There is fidelity to Christ, and there is friendship with the world. The great Scottish Reformer Robert Haldane wrote very powerfully about this:

> Many religious persons have a dread of controversy and wish truth to be stated without any reference to those who hold opposite errors. Controversy and a bad spirit are in their estimation synonymous terms; and strenuously to oppose what is wrong is considered as contrary to Christian meekness. Those who hold this opinion seem to overlook what every page of the New Testament lays before us. In all the history of the Lord Jesus Christ we never find him out of controversy.[4]

Haldane was referring to our Lord's life on this earth as recorded in the Gospels, and surely we find that He constantly and fearlessly battled those who perverted the truth. We, like the recipients of these letters in Revelation, are easily lulled into thinking that the purpose of our lives is peaceable comfort. But Jesus said, "Do not think that I have come to bring peace to the earth. I have not come to bring peace, but a sword" (Matt. 10:34). We want to be at peace with all, but it was not our Lord's intention that this would yet be so. Yes, we are to love everyone without exception, even our enemies, as a special mark of our unity with Christ. But Jesus says in Scripture that one of the worst things that could be said about any Christian, one of the most alarming signs of danger, is that he gets along with everyone: "Woe to you, when all people speak well of you, for so their fathers did to the false prophets" (Luke 6:26).

We must disabuse ourselves of the possibility of neutrality when it comes to matters of truth. There is fidelity to Christ, and there is friendship with the world.

We remember the emphasis on single-minded devotion to the Lord that highlighted the book of Deuteronomy. Jesus brings this same priority forward to the church in His demand for fidelity to truth. Similarly, Deuteronomy's call for holiness of life, moral and spiritual separation from the sinful world, is the next great emphasis in Jesus' letters to the churches. The Ephesians seem to stand for all today who boast of orthodoxy but do not combine it with a deep spirituality and love. "But I have this against you," Jesus stated, "that you have abandoned the love you had at first. Remember therefore from where you have fallen; repent, and do the works you did at first. If not, I will come to you and remove your lampstand from its place, unless you repent" (Rev. 2:4-5). Idolatry and sexual immorality come under attack in the letters to both Pergamum and Thyatira, coupled with the most severe warnings.

Jesus makes quite clear that trials suffered in these churches were His response to their gross immorality. This is not always the case, for our trials have a number of causes, often unclear to us. Yet here we see a warning many evangelical churches ought seriously to consider today (2:21-23). Just as Jesus holds churches responsible for the dissolute among them, so also He treasures those who have pursued purity, as seen in His remark to the church in Sardis: "Yet you have still a few names in Sardis, people who have not soiled their garments, and they will walk with me in white, for they are worthy" (3:4). Our Lord makes clear that we must persevere to the end in both matters of truth and moral godliness.

The third theme that dominates these letters is Jesus' demand for a fervent Christlike ministry in the church. It seems that He emphasizes both the gospel witness of the church and its ministry of mercy and justice, both of which call us back to Deuteronomic formation. Ephesus is called back to the works of her first days. We naturally think of the bold witness in Ephesus during apostolic times, when under the preaching of men like Paul and Apollos many were called out of darkness into the growing church. So powerful was the church's ministry in leading people out of gross immorality and idolatry that the idol makers sought their persecution. As Acts 17:6 says of those former days in the church, Christ's followers "turned the world upside down," and the church is to keep doing so today through its ministry of word and deed.

We see this same emphasis on works of ministry in the letters to Sardis and Laodicea, both of which have substituted a false worldly glory for the true glory of aggressive ministry in the name of the Lord. "I know your works," Jesus said to Sardis. "You have the reputation of being alive, but you are dead" (3:1). To Laodicea he warned, "Because you are lukewarm, and neither hot nor cold, I will spit you out of my mouth" (3:16).

All of these emphases—truth, holiness, and ministries of word and deed—take place in the context of great opposition and difficulty. The book of Revelation was delivered to those in the midst of persecution (see 1:9), and Jesus flatly points out to the church that reformation will take place in the face of opposition. Undoubtedly the most dangerous opposition is that which comes from within, and like the apostle Paul, Jesus reserves His sharpest language for those who teach falsely and lead His people astray. In each of the seven letters, our Lord promises great reward to "the one who conquers," making clear that those who serve Him faithfully must endure hostility and conflict in His service. "The one who conquers," he concludes, "I will grant him to sit with me on my throne, as I also conquered and sat down with my Father on his throne. He who has an ear, let him hear what the Spirit says to the churches" (Rev. 3:21-22).

Jesus flatly points out that reformation will take place in the
face of opposition. In each of the seven letters, He promises
great reward to "the one who conquers."

REFORMATA SEMPER REFORMANDA

Jesus says the churches are to hold fast to what they have received, while also engaging in a program of repentance in those areas where deformation has set in. This tells us that we are always to be reforming, both to preserve what we have and to counter the tendency toward unbelief and sin. "Hold fast what you have," he says, "so that no one may seize your crown" (3:11). "If you will not wake up, I will come like a thief, and you will not know at what hour I will come against you" (3:3). Reformation is both holding to and defending the heritage of our faith, as well as repenting of the various ways in which we have turned aside or forsaken the truth.

One of the key slogans of the sixteenth-century Protestant Reformation articulates this dual emphasis: *reformata semper reformanda*. That means *reformed, always reforming*. Our faith is received from prior generations, indeed from God by His Word and His providential working in history. We have that which was formed according to God's intention and then reformed again and again according to that Word by those who went before us. That is *reformata*—the past tense, the receptive sense of reformation. We must preserve and defend that sacred trust. But that implies an ongoing duty—namely, to continually regulate ourselves according to the Word, continually to purge out the leaven, continually to reform by combating deformation and doing the things we did at first. This is the ongoing, present, and active sense of reformation—*semper reformanda*. Together these two senses—holding on to what we have received from the past and carrying on that same work in the present—make up the charge of reformation.

Reformed, always reforming—an ongoing duty, to continually regulate ourselves according to the Word, continually to purge out the leaven, continually to reform by combating deformation and doing the things we did at first.

It is hard to overestimate the importance of this idea in our own time. To the great Reformers of previous generations, *reformata semper reformanda* meant that they constantly sought to scrutinize and conform themselves to the clear and sufficient revelation that is found in Scripture. Because of our sin and folly, we inevitably deviate from the pattern of God's Word; so ongoing reformation is needed in order to remember and repent and return to that which God has commanded in the Bible.

Unfortunately, like many of our historic expressions, this phrase is often used to defend something far different. People say that while "reformed" in the past tense, *reformata*, applies to what was done by a prior generation, "always reforming" in the present tense, *reformanda*, points to our freedom from the shackles of tradition. To them, *semper reformanda* is our mandate to revise and re-imagine the church according to the new insight of the times. Reformation, to these people, means innovation and necessary change; the Reformers made changes in their day, they argue, and we are making innovating changes today as well. An excellent example of this comes from the liberal Episcopal bishop Shelby Spong, who has vigorously denied and attacked virtually every tenet of historic and orthodox Christian teaching, but who nonetheless put out a book entitled *Here I Stand*. The title seeks to portray him as a new Luther, a true Reformer—even though he attacks and despises everything the Protestant Reformers stood for and, more importantly, what is taught in the Bible.

The Protestant Reformers would abhor such a version of events. It is vital to understand that they denied they were innovators, that theirs was a novel message and movement. Instead, they insisted they were merely correcting deformation as it had occurred over the years by returning to the biblical pattern of faith and practice. That is why leaders like John Calvin so often quoted the ancient church fathers, to show that their reformation was a return to what had been in the early days. This is especially why they made the Bible their only rule of faith and practice, so that their reforming work would be protected from human innovation and would be a consistent return to the Word of God.

In Jesus' letters we have not a hint of commendation for innovation or conformity to the changing world. As Almighty Lord, He calls His churches to triumph over the world, to perseverance in spite of the fierce opposition to true and saving Christianity. He depicts our situation in stark terms that few are willing to conceive of today. Those who will not reform will have their lampstand removed from its place, He says (2:5)—a judgment history records as ultimately visited upon these churches, which now consist only of mounds of rubble. Against those who fail to guard the truth Jesus "will come. . . . and wage war against them with the sword of my mouth" (2:16). Unless His people repent of falsehood and immorality and spiritual deadness, the Lord "who searches mind and heart. . . . will give to each of you as your works deserve" (2:23). He will "come like a thief" to those who fail to awake (3:3); to those who burn neither hot nor cold for Him, Jesus says, "I will spit you out of my mouth" (3:16). Here, then, is the call to reformation from the Lord of the church: "Those whom I love, I reprove and discipline, so be zealous and repent" (3:19).

As Almighty Lord, He calls His churches to triumph over the world. Here is His call to reformation: "Those whom I love, I reprove and discipline, so be zealous and repent" (3:19).

REMEMBER, REPENT

It can hardly be denied, with words like those from the mouth of our Lord Himself, that reformation is an urgent mandate for the people of God. Jesus Christ is the Great Reformer, calling on His people to hold fast to His name. His mandate is clear and compelling, and those who seek to obey can be sure of the help of the Holy Spirit Jesus sends.

Jesus calls us to hold fast to what we have received, and His key instruction to this effect is the command, "Remember." Twice in these letters Jesus calls on his people to remember. "Remember therefore from where you have fallen" (2:5), He tells the Ephesian believers. To the church at Smyrna, he commands, "Remember, then, what you received and heard. Keep it, and repent" (3:3).

We are reminded here of our starting point in the book of Deuteronomy, which sixteen times commands the people to remember. Israel was to remember standing before the Lord at Mount Sinai, hearing His very voice and receiving His law (4:10, NIV). They were to remember that they had been slaves in Egypt, but the Lord brought them out "with a mighty hand and an outstretched arm" (5:15). They were to remember how God humbled Pharaoh, then tested and humbled His people as well (7:18; 8:2). "But remember the LORD your God," says Deuteronomy 8:18 (NIV), "for it is he who gives you the ability to produce wealth, and so confirms his covenant, which he swore to your forefathers, as it is today."

Undoubtedly, the heart of Deuteronomy is what is called the *Shema*, the great commandment to confess and love the Lord, and this is coupled with most sober instructions about remembering the Lord:

"Hear, O Israel: The LORD our God, the LORD is one. You shall love the LORD your God with all your heart and with all your

soul and with all your might. And these words that I command
you today shall be on your heart. You shall teach them diligently
to your children, and shall talk of them when you sit in your
house, and when you walk by the way, and when you lie down,
and when you rise. You shall bind them as a sign on your hand,
and they shall be as frontlets between your eyes. You shall write
them on the doorposts of your house and on your gates. And
when the LORD *your God brings you into the land that he swore*
to your fathers . . . then take care lest you forget the LORD, *who*
brought you out of the land of Egypt, out of the house of slavery.

—6:4-12

What does this tell us but that loving God is most vitally manifested
by remembering Him, talking about Him with our children, binding our
very hearts with His Word. And if Israel was to remember the great
deliverance God brought through Moses, we Christians have a greater
deliverance and a greater Deliverer to remember. In his letter to Titus,
yet another reformation document in the New Testament, the apostle
Paul advises his protégé to remind the people of the great facts of their
redemption in Christ, to remember their bondage in the Egypt of their
sin and the salvation that is by grace alone through Jesus Christ:

At one time we too were foolish, disobedient, deceived and
enslaved by all kinds of passions and pleasures. We lived in mal-
ice and envy, being hated and hating one another. But when the
kindness and love of God our Savior appeared, he saved us, not
because of righteous things we had done, but because of his
mercy. He saved us through the washing of rebirth and renewal
by the Holy Spirit, whom he poured out on us generously
through Jesus Christ our Savior, so that, having been justified
by his grace, we might become heirs having the hope of eternal
life. This is a trustworthy saying. And I want you to stress these
things, so that those who have trusted in God may be careful to
devote themselves to doing what is good. These things are
excellent and profitable for everyone.

—3:3-8, NIV

Notice Paul's logic here: By remembering the doctrines of grace, the
spiritual facts and doctrines of our salvation in Christ, God's people will

be motivated to faith and obedience. Surely this is a mandate for biblical, doctrinal teaching that constantly reminds Christians of the Gospel—that is, the good news of our exodus in Christ, from bondage to salvation. So, too, does this call us to the faithful administration of the sacraments, which Jesus told us to observe "in remembrance of me" (1 Cor. 11:25).

This means that if our churches are going to experience reformation today, it will be through a rediscovery of God's Word. Ours must be a day like Josiah's, when the lost book is brought forth into the light. Superficially there may seem to be little in common between Josiah's time and ours. Our Bibles are not hidden in a corner of the church building but are prominently displayed for all to see. Yet below the surface we see that the Bible no longer serves as the church's guide for faith and life. For all its visibility, God's Word is perhaps as lost today in the church as in the dark days of Judah's wicked kings.

In a book written shortly before his death, James Montgomery Boice identified this as perhaps the chief problem in the church today. He wrote: "It is possible to believe that the Bible is the inerrant Word of God, the only infallible rule of faith and practice, and yet to neglect it and effectually repudiate it just because we think that it is not sufficient to today's tasks and that other things need to brought in to accomplish what is needed."[5] Because of this, our churches are governed by the principles of therapeutic psychology, business practice, and increasingly by New Age mysticism instead of the Bible. What we need so greatly today is to heed the call of our risen Lord, who calls to us with the double-edged sword of his mouth, "Remember." May we therefore stand forth in our time like Hilkiah the high priest, delivering God's Word into the hands of a new generation of Josiahs.

What did Josiah do when he received the Law and realized its generations of neglect? He tore his robes in lament before the Lord and made provision for the Scriptures to be taught and put into practice. This is the command Jesus couples with that to remember: *Repent.* "Remember therefore from where you have fallen; repent, and do the works you did at first" (Rev. 2:5). "Remember, therefore, what you have received and heard; obey it, and repent" (Rev. 3:3, NIV).

We need to recover John's vision of our Lord in all His sovereign power and glory, in the place of the chummy Jesus of our own making who so gladly accepts whatever we propose in His name. There is not a church today that ought to be able to read John's description of the Reforming Lord amongst the candlesticks without fear and trembling because of failure and sin. Just seeing the exalted Jesus caused John the apostle to fall at His feet as though dead. The seven churches of these letters, in what is modern-day Turkey, are no more. It was in earnest that Jesus warned, "If you do not repent, I will come to you and remove your lampstand from its place" (Rev. 2:5, NIV). But Jesus said to John, after he had shown his repentance, "Do not be afraid" (Rev. 1:17). We too should have no fear of Jesus, if we are willing to repent. What we should fear is not His gracious rule, but rather our hard and foolish hearts, lest we should be unwilling to repent and therefore cause our Lord to judge and chastise us.

Jesus never merely threatens—He also woos His purchased bride with sweet promises, and these ought especially to enliven us today for the work of reformation in His church. To those who press on in truth and in love He says, "I will grant to eat of the tree of life, which is in the paradise of God" (2:7). Those who follow Him to the end "will not be hurt by the second death" (2:11). Jesus adds His gift of "the hidden manna" and "a white stone" (2:17). He promises glory to those who conquer: "And I will give him the morning star" (2:28). For following Him to the end, reforming the church and our lives in persevering faith, Jesus promises "white garments" and our names forever written in "the book of life" (3:5). He will make each of his faithful "a pillar in the temple of my God" (3:12). Concluding these seven striking letters, each of which contains a particular command to reformation, Jesus draws us to Himself, saying, "Behold, I stand at the door and knock. If anyone hears my voice and opens the door, I will come in to him and eat with him, and he with me. The one who conquers, I will grant him to sit with me on my throne, as I also conquered and sat down with my Father on his throne. He who has an ear, let him hear what the Spirit says to the churches" (3:20-22). This is not salvation by works, but rather the spiritual reality of blessing in the kingdom bought with the blood of Christ and entered into by faith in His name.

Notice, however, that these incentives are spiritual and not temporal. Perhaps this is the great challenge of our times, the test God gives to us as once He did to Israel in their Exodus journey. Is it success we desire, defined in worldly terms and achieved by worldly means and methods? Or is it faithfulness to God, even in the midst of present weakness and trials, with an eternal hope of blessing yet to come? "He who has an ear," Jesus calls, "let him hear what the Spirit says to the churches. To him who overcomes, I will give the right to eat from the tree of life, which is in the paradise of God" (Rev. 2:7, NIV).

If what we long for as Christians is the spiritual blessing that flows from the grace of Christ, then surely we will find all we ever could want or need in Him. If we will seek first His kingdom and His righteousness, we surely will take our place among the faithful of all ages, joining with them in the song of joy. The book of Revelation goes on to show multitudes of God's faithful, dressed in white and bearing palm branches, singing out in praise: "Salvation belongs to our God, who sits on the throne, and to the Lamb" (Rev. 7:10). This is the recompense for those who would stand with reformers of every age, men and women sacrificially committed to obeying the Word of God—not seeking money or power or fame or glory as counted in this world, but rather fellowship with God in His glory and light eternally shining down from His throne. Isaac Watts memorializes our hope in the words of a great hymn, and may our chief ambition simply be to find ourselves within this beloved scene:

> How bright these glorious spirits shine!
>   Whence all their white array?
> How came they to the blissful seats of everlasting day?
> Lo! These are they from suff'ring great who came to realms of
> light,
> And in the blood of Christ have washed those robes
>   which shine so bright.

> Now, with triumphal palms, they stand before the throne on high,
> And serve the God they love, amidst the glories of the sky.
> His presence fills each heart with joy, tunes every mouth to sing;
> By day, by night, the sacred courts with glad hosannas ring.

> Among pastures green He'll lead his flock where
>   living streams appear;
> And God the Lord from every eye shall wipe off every tear.
> To Him who sits upon the throne, the God whom we adore,
> And to the Lamb that once was slain be glory evermore!

NOTES

Preface

1. For a copy of the Cambridge Declaration or for more information on the Alliance of Confessing Evangelicals, you may want to visit its website at www.AllianceNet.org.

Introduction

1. D. Martyn Lloyd-Jones, "Remembering the Reformation," from *Knowing the Times: Addresses Delivered on Various Occasions 1942-1977* (Carlisle, PA: Banner of Truth, 1989), 94.
2. J. C. Ryle, *No Uncertain Sound* (Carlisle, PA: Banner of Truth, 1978), 52-53.
3. Charles H. Spurgeon, *Lectures to My Students* (Grand Rapids, MI: Zondervan, n.d.), 230-233.

Chapter One

1. Christopher Wright, *Deuteronomy* (Peabody, MA: Hendrickson, 1996), 22.
2. Ibid., 55.
3. *Webster's Ninth Collegiate Dictionary* (Springfield, MA: Merriam-Webster, 1984).

Chapter Two

1. Christopher Wright, *Deuteronomy* (Peabody, MA: Hendrickson, 1996), 280.
2. Raymond Brown, *The Message of Deuteronomy* (Downers Grove, IL: InterVarsity, 1993), 269.
3. Peter C. Craigie, *The Book of Deuteronomy* (Grand Rapids, MI: Eerdmans, 1976), 341.

Chapter Three

1. Rick Warren, *The Purpose-Driven Church* (Grand Rapids, MI: Zondervan, 1995), 207-238.

Chapter Four

1. D. Martyn Lloyd-Jones, *Old Testament Evangelistic Sermons* (Carlisle, PA: Banner of Truth, 1995), 152.
2. Ibid., 146.
3. Russell H. Dilday, *1, 2 Kings* (Dallas: Word, 1987), 164.

Chapter Five

1. J. Alec Motyer, *The Prophecy of Isaiah* (Downers Grove, IL: InterVarsity, 1993), 82.
2. John N. Oswalt, *The Book of Isaiah, Chapters 1-39* (Grand Rapids, MI: Eerdmans, 1986), 194.

Chapter Six

1. Philip G. Ryken, *Courage to Stand* (Wheaton, IL: Crossway, 1998), 58-59.
2. Ibid., 65-67.
3. Geerhardus Vos, "Jeremiah's Plaint and Its Answer," *The Princeton Theological Review* 26 (1928): 481-495. Cited from Vos, *Redemptive History and Biblical Interpretation*, ed. Richard B. Gaffin, Jr. (Phillipsburg, NJ: Presbyterian & Reformed, 1980).
4. J. Gordon McConville, *Grace in the End: A Study in Deuteronomic Theology* (Grand Rapids, MI: Zondervan, 1993), 137.

Chapter Seven

1. S. K. Mosiman and D. F. Payne, "Jehoshaphat," in *The International Standard Bible Encyclopedia*, 4 vols., gen. ed. Geoffrey W. Bromiley (Grand Rapids, MI: Eerdmans, 1982), 2:978.
2. Peter Jones, *Gospel Truth, Pagan Lies* (Enumclaw, WA: Winepress, 1999), 17, 39.
3. John Calvin, *The Minor Prophets*, 5 vols. (Carlisle, PA: Banner of Truth, 1986), 1:452.
4. Robert Godfrey, *Pleasing God in Our Worship* (Wheaton, IL: Crossway Books, 1999), 11.
5. Ibid., 15.
6. James Montgomery Boice, *Whatever Happened to the Gospel of Grace?* (Wheaton, IL: Crossway Books, 2001), 84.
7. James Montgomery Boice, *Ephesians* (Grand Rapids, MI: Zondervan, 1988), 86.
8. Martyn Lloyd-Jones, *Growing in the Spirit* (Wheaton, IL: Crossway Books, 1988), 138.
9. Robert Godfrey, "The Myth of Influence," *ModernReformation*, Vol. 7, No. 5, Sept./Oct. 1998, 19.

Chapter Eight

1. David F. Wells, *No Place for Truth* (Grand Rapids, MI: Eerdmans, 1993), 169.

Chapter Nine

1. D. Martyn Lloyd-Jones, *Old Testament Evangelistic Sermons* (Carlisle, PA: Banner of Truth Trust, 1995), 38-39.
2. John Calvin, *The Mystery of Godliness* (Morgan, PA: Soli Deo Gloria, 1999), 60-61.

Chapter Ten

1. Dennis E. Johnson, *Triumph of the Lamb* (Phillipsburg, NJ: Presbyterian & Reformed, 2001), 63.
2. Vern S. Poythress, *The Returning King: A Guide to the Book of Revelation* (Phillipsburg, NJ: Presbyterian & Reformed, 2000), 83.
3. Johnson, *Triumph of the Lamb*, 71.
4. Cf. D. Martyn Lloyd-Jones, "Remembering the Reformation," from *Knowing the Times: Addresses Delivered on Various Occasions 1942-1977* (Carlisle, PA: Banner of Truth, 1989), ix.
5. James Montgomery Boice, *Whatever Happened to the Gospel of Grace?* (Wheaton, IL: Crossway, 2000), 72.

SCRIPTURE INDEX

Master's
Counseling

Visiting days at Antioc
in Keene, N

Tuesdays, February
8:30 A

- Visit classes • Mee...
- Receive information on...
- Discover which p

CLINICAL MENTAL HEALTH ...
(optional concentration in
DANCE/MOVEMENT THERA...
MARRIAGE AND FAMILY THE...

|||...||.||..||...|...||...|||...|||...||...|...||...||

General Index